The organization
reveals the singul
disciplinary achievements,
as well as the rich plurality of
shared topics. A key aspect
of the work is its emphasis on
transdisciplinary practices that
react to our ever-changing global
forces. We are fortunate to
have so many talented students
and faculty devote their time to
making the GSD the world's
leading institution for developing
alternative and exemplary forms
of practice that promise to shape
our future environments.

This book is a token of that
promise.

MOHSEN MOSTAFAVI
DEAN
ALEXANDER AND VICTORIA WILEY PROFESSOR OF DESIGN

GSD Platform 3

Harvard University
Graduate School of Design

Platform 3 considers the expanded boundaries of the Harvard University Graduate School of Design. It features not only selections of work produced at the GSD during the 2009–2010 academic year, but also the potential of that work to address broader questions and inform global initiatives.

Whether exploring the potential of a new technology, redefining a typology, or engaging a community on the other side of the globe, the lines of inquiry beginning at the GSD consistently indicate relevance to larger social, cultural, and spatial questions. To understand the scope of this potential impact, the work is framed with one simple question.

By asking, "What can design do?" we have identified five actions that describe the ability of Architecture, Landscape Architecture, and Urban Planning and Design at the GSD to reach beyond their immediate contexts and out into the world:

Instigate Evolution
Describe Identity
Construct Equality
Negotiate Growth
Imagine New Futures

The range and definition of these actions is tested and demonstrated through the work of a representative collection of studios, lectures, seminars, symposia, colloquia, conferences, thesis projects, and student research across disciplines throughout the school. The core studios—the foundational design research at the GSD—are presented here in sequence to show the progression from the first semester through to the fourth.

Each of these featured entries expands the limits of design and invites us to reconsider the role of the architect, the landscape architect, the urban planner and designer in defining the world of the future.

EMILY WAUGH
LECTURER IN LANDSCAPE ARCHITECTURE

NEW TRAJECTORIES
CONVERGENT FLUX: K

ACCELERATED DENSITY

If urban density evolves based on cultural, economic, and social aspects, what happens when the progression of these factors is so accelerated that a radical disjunction occurs, instead of a gradual shift? In roughly the last half-century, the urban population has reached unprecedented concentrations: 50 percent of South Koreans now live in Seoul and its satellites, which occupy only 12 percent of the nation's land. This story, however, cannot simply be told as a journey from low-rise to high-rise living. In fact, Seoul has the lowest physical density for the highest density of people per hectare. Instead, unique and intensely hybridized typologies are evolving from the limitations that density presents. And as the growth of concentrated urbanism centered around Seoul reaches its physical and psychological limits, new approaches to de-centralization are emerging that go beyond sprawl, suburbanization, and the myth of individuality to posit new visions of the collective.

TOPOGRAPHICAL SYNTA

When extreme topography defines a region, how do modern techniques of standardized production overwhelm a specific geographical condition? Korea is 70 percent mountainous, with more than 90 percent of its population compressed into urbanized areas that cover less than 10 percent of the land. This tension between the nation's proclivity for increasing development pressure has often resulted in the flattening of natural areas. Yet a systematic understanding of the significance of topography has periodically entered the Korean consciousness. Centuries of abstract representational mappings of landforms have enabled a responsive relationship between the people and their environment and impacts over the control of the landscape through perspectival space. The historical understanding of topography as a highly nuanced yet systematic language, rather than a series of particularized moments, is giving rise to design approaches that explore reciprocal relationships between the built environment and Korea's challenging topographic condition.

STOCK-PILE

Instigate Evolution

The explorations in this chapter demonstrate the transformative role of design in the evolution of a typology, a place, a city, or an approach. Through architecture, landscape architecture, and urban planning and design, we can give new relevance and function to existing things, revive urban centers, and create a bridge between past and future.

At some point in your life as a professional, you are going to be concerned with the location of your creative thought. Because you're not going to write a single novel, you're going to write many, many pieces, and you have to have a conceptual underpinning of that work.

My practice as an architect in some way started with the school we did in California, and I remember when Richard Weinstein, the ex-dean of UCLA and I were walking through it, he looked at me and he said, "Thom, this is your first piece of work, and it's the first time the social act and the aesthetic act were integrated." He was right. And in this case, it was extremely interesting because, from the very beginning, the primary interest was not architecture in the formal sense. It was how architecture participates in education, how it participates in increasing the inquisitiveness of the student, how it operates on their mind, and in some lasting effect that in this case, it was parallel to an idea that we've been working with for twenty years having to do with earth augmentation and the notion of the site as it becomes very active in the project, which started way back in 1985 with the competition in Vienna and another one in Paris.

Right after the school we were working on a bank in Austria and it was clear here that we were discussing an architecture that's relational. There was an instinctual sense that projects weren't objects. They were connections of objects, and what I was interested in was the connectivity and the relational aspect of the work versus the thing itself as an object.

What I'm interested in is the type of energy and the kind of power that comes from the relationship of these various parts. And as it's been developing over the last thirty years, it's moved more and more from a compositional, intentional, purposeful, a priori idea to something that's much more casual, much more associative versus specific in its relationship to geometry, and loaded with purposeful accidents.

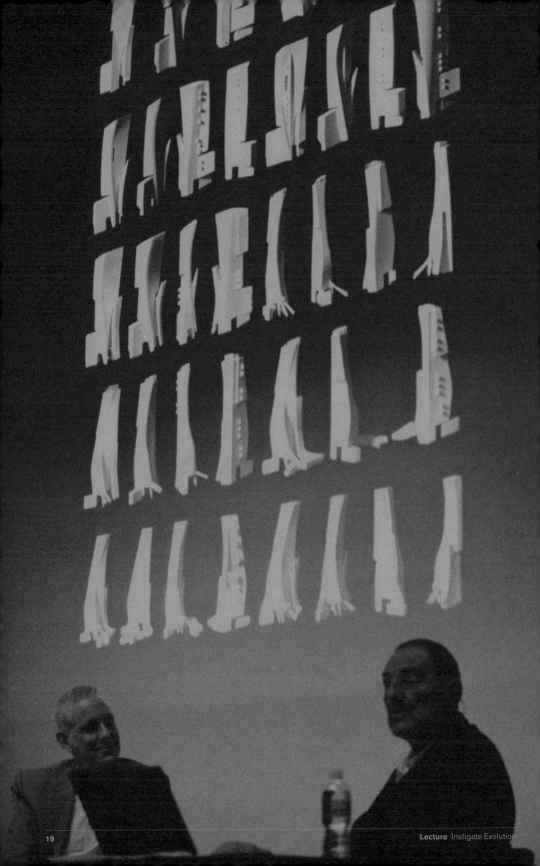

There was still the opportunity we've talked about from when I started with the school: this notion of augmentation of land. You actually occupy this new condition between one ground and another ground, understanding that all of them are, more or less, manmade, that there's no such thing as nature, that nature itself is being attacked, and that in fact, today, we look at the artificial; the construction of nature as the activity.

This carried through to the Caltrans building when at that time, the crinkled language as it touched the ground was a continuation of an interpretation of the ground as an idea, and I've been preoccupied with that since my first work. I have also been working with surface/solid since I was a kid. The same thing keeps reiterating, it differentiates. You'll also see pieces left out, or unfinished.

A conversation I've been having, again, for 30 years. Everything is left unfinished. If you look at literally every building I've ever done, you'll see it's been left in fragments.

And then, last, a project that I'm working on in Shanghai right now. We have started using a combatorial technique where I can add various components and look at those in their relationship to one another, make decisions in terms of solving the endless number of contingencies that we're asked to solve as architects, and do it within a controlled method. Out of that comes the convention of plans.

There is absolutely nothing I'm interested in anymore that I can draw or I can preconceive. If I can preconceive it, it is boring before it even goes down on the page because I already knew it. I am really looking for a way of developing an architecture that is beyond my own capacities, that can lead me to something new.

COMPUTATIONAL DESIGN AND MATERIAL GESTALT - PERFORMATIVE WOOD: RECIPROCITIES OF FORM, MATERIAL, STRUCTURE, AND ENVIRONMENT

OPTION STUDIO   ACHIM MENGES

"The manifest form—that which appears—is the result of a computational interaction between internal rules and external (morphogenetic) pressures that, themselves, originate in other adjacent forms (ecology). The (pre-concrete) internal rules comprise, in their activity, an embedded form, what is today clearly understood and described by the term algorithm." —Sanford Kwinter

This studio investigated the largely unexplored field of computational design research that aims at integrating processes of form generation and materialization.

Contrary to the still predominant modes of computer aided design in use in today's architectural practice, computational design externalizes the relation between form, formation, and information. This enables an understanding of form, material, structure, and environment not as separate elements, but rather as complex, co-evolving, reciprocal interrelations that can be embedded in and explored through integral computational design processes. The aim of the studio was to explore such an alternative, morphogenetic approach to architectural design, which unfolds specific material gestalt and related performative capacities without differentiating between processes of computational form generation and physical materialization.

The studio began with the hands-on development of material systems. Wood was chosen as the common starting point, with the aim of investigating how one of the oldest construction materials can now be understood and employed as a natural, adaptable, high-performance fiber composite material. Step by step the material system's characteristics, manufacturing constraints and assembly logics, as well as its interaction with external environmental influences and forces, were embedded in a generative computational design framework. Studio work concluded with the development and production of material prototypes, functioning as vehicles to speculate about the repercussions of an integral computational design approach on architecture as a material practice.

The studio was supported by a number of workshops that introduced the related computational design tools as well as the concepts of material systems and algorithmic design thinking.

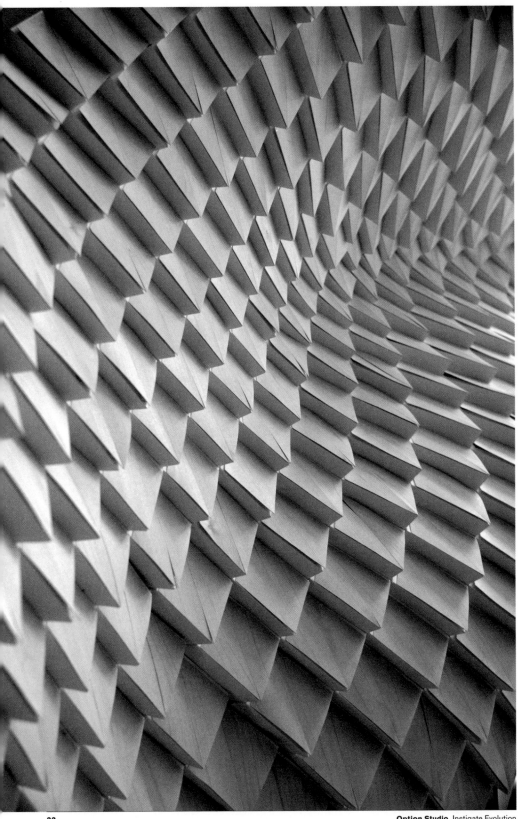

Steam Bending Members

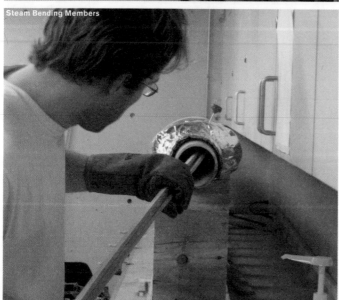

Steam Bending Members

JEFFREY NIEMASZ, JON SARGENT, LAURA VIKLUND

Prototype

Transparency

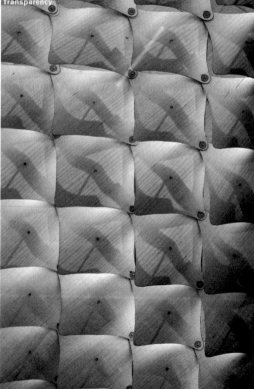

Module Assembly Diagram

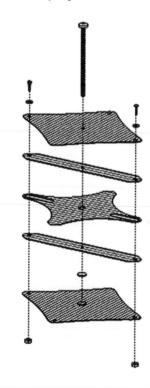

STAGING GROUND:
STRUCTURAL LOGISTICS
AND ECOLOGICAL INFRASTRUCTURE
IN THE SACRAMENTO -
SAN JOAQUIN RIVER DELTA

MLA THESIS | ANDREW TENBRINK

ADVISORS: CHRIS REED, CHARLES WALDHEIM

Emerging practices in the field of landscape architecture have undergone a shift in their methods of engaging the site. This movement has begun to break through the qualities of the static master plan, altering and extending the relationship between the designer to the site, client and public. Infrastructure has established itself as the primary medium with which this shift has occurred. In a 2009 report by the American Society of Civil Engineers, the nation's infrastructures were concluded to be at a pivot point of failure, requiring more than $2 trillion to repair. The project seeks to establish a structural infrastructure within the Sacramento-San Joaquin Delta, hybridized with the ecologies and logistics of water transport between the delta and agricultural polder. This infrastructural piece fosters a public interaction with these operations, making visible the methods of water control and registering the changes therein through a new recreational ecology. The agency of infrastructure must move beyond its traditional myopic mode and embrace a new hybrid state.

From Estuary to Infrastructure

aquatic habitat

285,250 ac
aquatic habitat
323,500 ac

140

210 *number of alien species within the delta*

SAVE THE DELTA

5MAF
1967
6MAF
1980
7MAF
1985
8MAF
1990
9MAF
1995
8MAF
1998
9MAF
2000
9MAF
2001

Apple Water and Population Increases

Structure

PORTS OF STOCKTON

PORTS OF OAKLAND

PORT OF SAN FRANCISCO

LEVEE FAILURES SINCE 1900

NOTE: Exact data not available prior to 1900, so all levee failures prior to 1900 are shown above.

1900   1910   1920   1930   1940   1950   1960   1970   1980   1990   2000

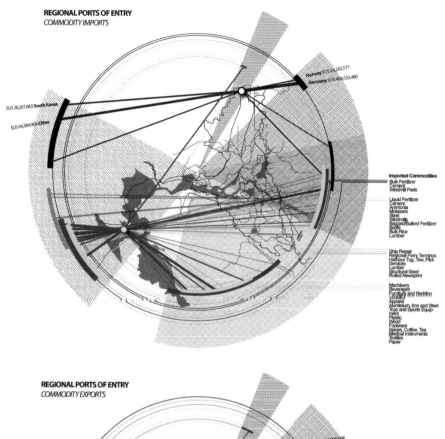

REGIONAL PORTS OF ENTRY
COMMODITY IMPORTS

Norway $US 24,242,571
Germany $US 404,532,480

$US 28,207,063 South Korea

$US 64,384,908 China

Imported Commodities
Bulk Fertilizer
Cement
Windmill Parts

Liquid Fertilizer
Cement
Ammonia
Molasses
Steel
Windmills
Bagged/Bulked Fertilizer
Battle
Bulk Rice
Lumber

Ship Repair
Regional Ferry Terminus
Harbour Tug, Tow, Pilot
Services
Lumber
Structural Steel
Rolled Newsprint

Machinery
Beverages
Furniture and Bedding
Clothing
Apparel
Aluminium, Iron and Steel
Toys and Sports Equip-
ment
Plastic
Wood
Footwear
Spices, Coffee, Tea
Medical Instruments
Textiles
Paper

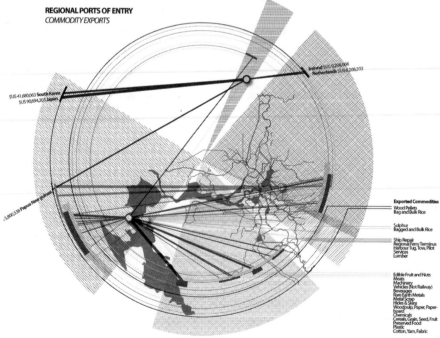

REGIONAL PORTS OF ENTRY
COMMODITY EXPORTS

Ireland $US 9,206,066
Netherlands $US 64,208,393

$US 41,680,063 South Korea
$US 90,694,203 Japan

, 5,800,538 Papua New Guinea

Exported Commodities
Wood Pellets
Bag and Bulk Rice

Sulphur
Bagged and Bulk Rice

Ship Repair
Regional Ferry Terminus
Harbour Tug, Tow, Pilot
Services
Lumber

Edible Fruit and Nuts
Meats
Machinery
Vehicles (Not Railway)
Beverages
Rare Earth Metals
Metal Scrap
Hides & Skins
Woodpulp, Paper, Paper-
board
Chemicals
Cereals, Grain, Seed, Fruit
Preserved Food
Plastic
Cotton, Yarn, Fabric

Detail of Water Siphon Mechanism Enabling Ephemeral Plant Growth

Levee Entrance into the Inhabitable Infrastructure

Model

Thesis Instigate Evolution

A LIVING ARCHIVE: INHABITATING IDIOSYNCRATIC EXHIBITIONS OF MEMORY IN A NEW GEOGRAPHY OF CURIOSITY

JAMES T. KELLEY PRIZE | MEGAN FORNEY PANZANO

ADVISOR: MARIANA IBANEZ

Megan's thesis focuses on the relationship between personal collecting and curation in the domestic realm. This relationship exposes two conditions—a rising tendency of the general population to over-consume, and the value that personal objects have in defining personal identity. The architectural implications of these conditions are explored through the proposal of a new type, a part-storage, part-house, part-museum module and the spatial potential of their integration.

While the research traces the history of personal collections and their evolution into elaborate archival systems, it is the re-appropriation of archiving as a personal enterprise that produces a significant typological invention. One in which the dynamic nature of the act of collecting contaminates all spaces of use, their programmatic specificity, and tectonic definition.

—Mariana Ibanez

This thesis proposes the design of a new architectural type—a living archive. The project recognizes the cultural compulsion to collect in the U.S., and investigates how this practice should transform the existing typologies of the home and the archive within an emergent American landscape of storage.

This new architectural intervention experiments with the home as the activated site for engagement with a collection by reintegrating object curation with the idiosyncratic habits of living to create a dynamic archive.

This new type proposes the return of the classification of objects, as a tool for the structuring of knowledge, to its roots in the interactive lab of the home while also offering a space for the exhibition and encoding of personal memory.

The goal of this project is to better spatially capture and project the dynamism, emotion, and discursive potentials intrinsic to the process of personal collecting.

Longitudinal Section through Living Archive Unit

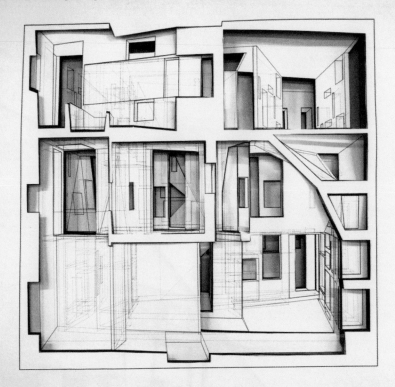

Transverse Section through Living Archive Unit

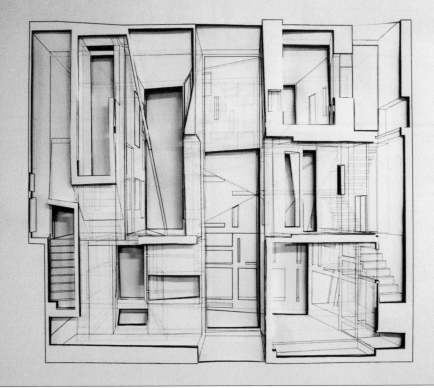

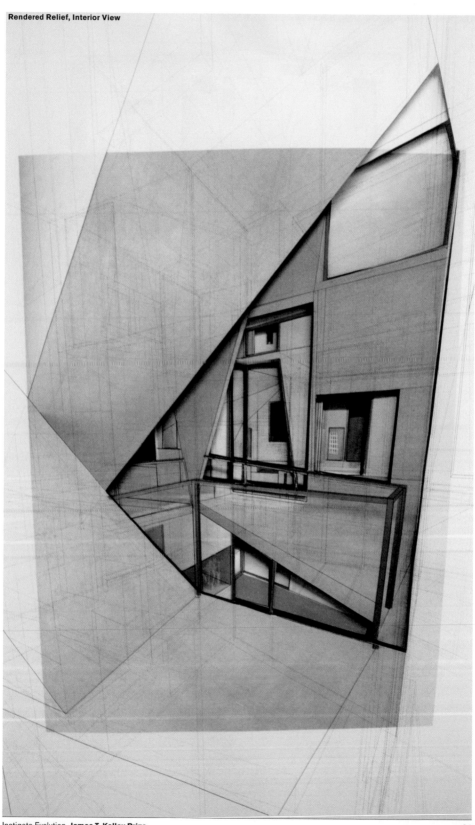

MIES IMMERSION:
THE PERFORMANCE SHED

OPTION STUDIO   GEORGE LEGENDRE

Halfway between the dominant discourse of programmatic freedom and the alleged over-determination and futility of form-giving, this studio pursues its critical return to form. Contrary to the notion of shape (with which it is sometimes confused), here form is understood as a syntactic, procedural and, increasingly, technical proposition whose disciplinary autonomy parallels the study of language in the age of structuralism or the development of object-oriented programming in the contemporary software industry.

Mies Applications:

In keeping with the line of enquiry initiated at the GSD last year with the Singapore-hosted option studio Rising Masses, we will expand the scope of our preliminary design explorations to the production of formal analytic models, later to be incorporated into programmatic architectural proposals for downtown Chicago.

Most importantly we will scavenge history to reformulate our essentially instrumental ideas in relation to the high modernist project of Ludwig Mies van der Rohe (1886-1969). From the recent completion of the McCormick Tribune Campus Center at IIT by OMA to the major show curated by Phyllis Lambert in 2001, the ongoing rediscovery of Mies has been gathering pace. Critically, Mies's ethos is still in some way at the root of our problems. None of the wild formalism practiced globally in 2009 would have been possible without his original rejection of locality, program, and typological individuation, abetted by his use of seemingly totalizing grids, reiterative frames, and serialized prefabrication. Mies's architecture is mostly restrained and orthogonal, and ours mostly exuberant and groovy, but if you disregard that detail, pound for pound the two strategies are strictly equivalent. Having foretold our ambition to formulate a root-less contemporary sensibility, Mies is now in need of an explicit reactualization.

JAE MIN HA AND SEONG SEOK KO

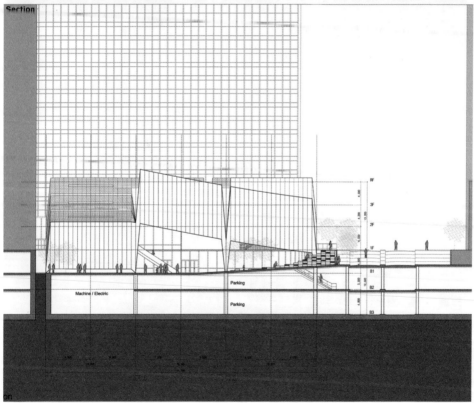

Section

Machine / Electric

Parking

Parking

RF

3F

2F

1F

B1

B2

B3

GENEVIEVE MACNEIL

West-Facing Section

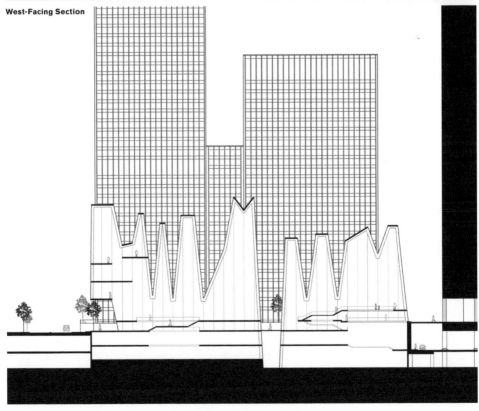

Uncoiled Walls

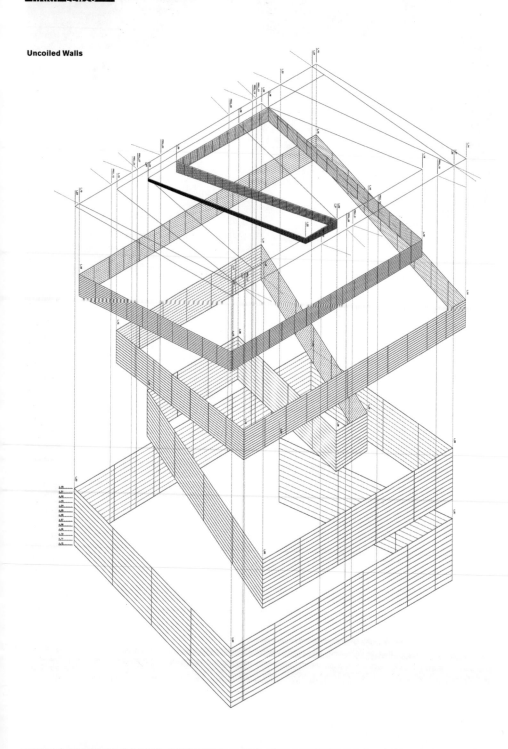

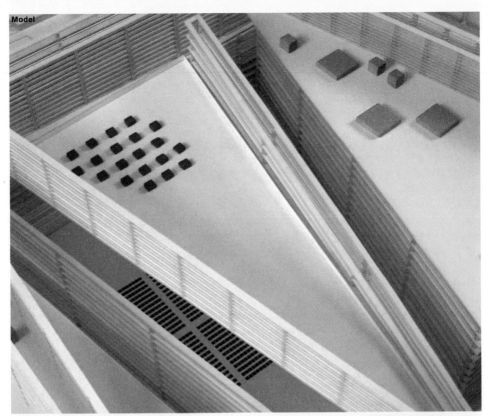
Model

Model

KPF Travelling Fellowship Instigate Evolution

HARVARD GSD COLLOQUIA
ON LANDSCAPE:
THE FUTURE OF HISTORY

COLLOQUIUM | CHARLES WALDHEIM INTRODUCTORY REMARKS

SPEAKERS:
STEPHEN DANIELS, DIANNE HARRIS, RACHAEL ZIADY DELUE,
VITTORIA DI PALMA, GEORGES FARHAT,
RAFFAELLA FABIANI GIANNETTO, JOHN DIXON HUNT,
MARK LAIRD

We are here this evening to inaugurate a new venue; a new space in which we hope to be able to frame discussions around questions attendant to landscape as a discipline. In the department, and in the school we have had many venues in which we could discuss landscape architecture as a profession, as a medium of design, and a range of other topics related to ecology and technology, but it has become increasingly clear over the last several months in our discussions that it would be helpful to have a venue specifically dedicated to the disciplinary discourse of landscape.

Over the next several weeks, we will be hosting an evening series that we're calling "The Harvard GSD Colloquia on Landscape." We are using this new format to enter into what we hope will be a stimulating set of discussions about the state of landscape history in the English language. We are interested to use this new venue to engage in a discussion of landscape history and its status and to try to gain a broader perspective on the history, present configuration, and future potential of landscape historiography. This topic at this time has much to do with the particular institutional context that we inhabit, but also, certain transitions in the field. We're standing, now, in the wake of John Dixon Hunt's retirement at Penn, the passing of Denis Cosgrove, and a host of other retirements and transitions that one could identify around people who have been central to the construction of landscape history over the course of the last decades.

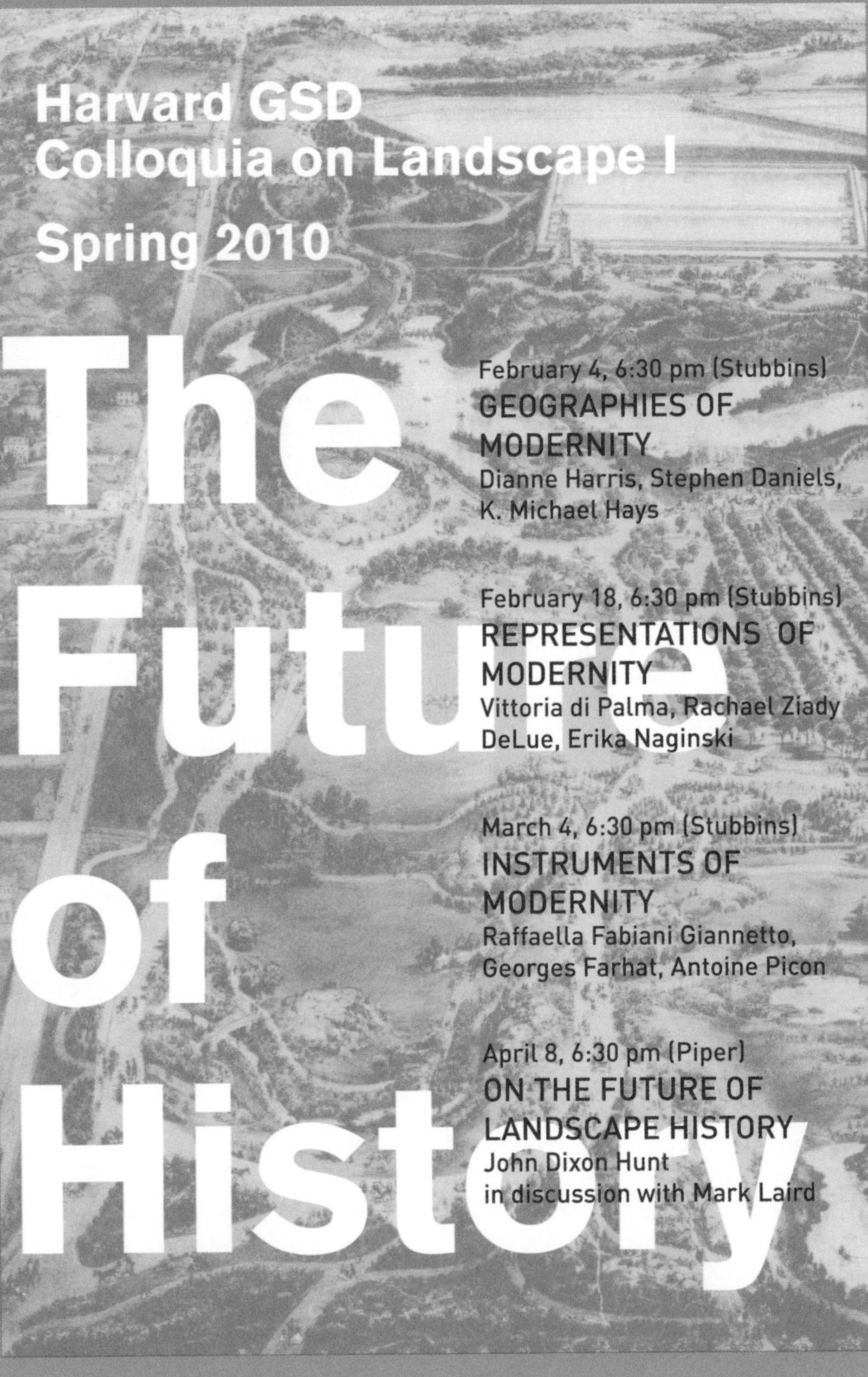

Harvard GSD
Colloquia on Landscape I
Spring 2010

The Future of History

February 4, 6:30 pm (Stubbins)
GEOGRAPHIES OF MODERNITY
Dianne Harris, Stephen Daniels, K. Michael Hays

February 18, 6:30 pm (Stubbins)
REPRESENTATIONS OF MODERNITY
Vittoria di Palma, Rachael Ziady DeLue, Erika Naginski

March 4, 6:30 pm (Stubbins)
INSTRUMENTS OF MODERNITY
Raffaella Fabiani Giannetto, Georges Farhat, Antoine Picon

April 8, 6:30 pm (Piper)
ON THE FUTURE OF LANDSCAPE HISTORY
John Dixon Hunt in discussion with Mark Laird

John Dixon Hunt (left) and Mark Laird (right)

The department of landscape architecture here at the GSD has had a particular focus on the history of the modernist landscape. This project has been fueled by the desire to construct landscape history as a kind of disciplinary surrogate to the well-established history of stylistic modernism in architecture. While this has been a valuable project, our focus this evening and in the coming weeks will be less on modernism as a stylistic category and more completely on landscape as a medium associated with modernity as a set of social, economic, and technological transformations.

Landscape has had a history of being a rather promiscuous discipline. It comes from different sources, it signifies in different ways, and that relative instability or insecurity manifests itself in different forms.

We are taking the approach, in this context and in others, that rather than being a position of weakness, that kind of multifarious, multifaceted condition—that promiscuity of the field—is, in fact, a great, inherent strength. If we could position it as a strength, we might, in fact, be able to multiply and pluralize the thinking in and around the field.

There are so many real pressures about disciplinarity, but one of the virtues of landscape is that it is not just something you look at but it is a lens on the wider world. It isn't owned by any one discipline.

—Stephen Daniels

ARCHITECTURE I

CORE

INSTRUCTORS: PRESTON SCOTT COHEN, YAEL EREL, DANIELLE ETZLER, ERIC HÖWELER, INGEBORG ROCKER, ELIZABETH WHITTAKER, CAMERON WU   FALL 2009

The first of a four-semester sequence of design studios introduced students to the practice of architectural design, discussing the theoretical principles on which such practice is based.

PROJECT #1: ELEVATOR INTERVENTION The program for this project was to add an elevator enclosed in a continuous vertical passage and to reconfigure the stairs, thresholds, rooms, and other constituent elements affected by the intervention without eliminating any of them.

PROJECT #2: LODGED HOUSE The goal was to design a flexible space, capable of serving either domestic, work, study, or other private uses, in a new house to be located in a space between two existing, nearly identical houses. A problem to be solved was the likelihood that the proposal would create difficulties for the adjacent buildings, blocking several windows and making some rooms unusable.

PROJECT #3: THE HIDDEN ROOM This project involved designing a group of five rooms, one of which appeared hidden from the other four. The program required providing a means of access to the hidden room while controlling the degree to which the room was vulnerable to disclosure.

PROJECT #4: THE PLAN FROM WITHOUT Concepts as represented in the plans included: a system and an anomaly posing as a duality in plan; clustered pairs/dyads of rooms and walls that appeared organized in an overlapping and nonhierarchical arrangement; four spaces that appeared to be strictly separated from the "outside," composed of both air and earth; and two similar trapezoidal plans stacked one atop the other that appeared to define four rooms.

PROJECT #5: LOCK BUILDING The project was about movement in time and space, actualized mechanically. The program was a building, parts of which were connected to and moved with the gate of a boat lock. The building was required to enable continuous pedestrian passage across the lock when the gate was shut and nautical passage through the lock when the gate was open. The project was about the development of two crossing, mutually disruptive paths.

Bridging the Gap

EMMET TRUXES

Rate of Movement

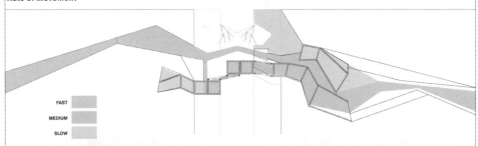

FAST

MEDIUM

SLOW

Separation of Path and Tempo

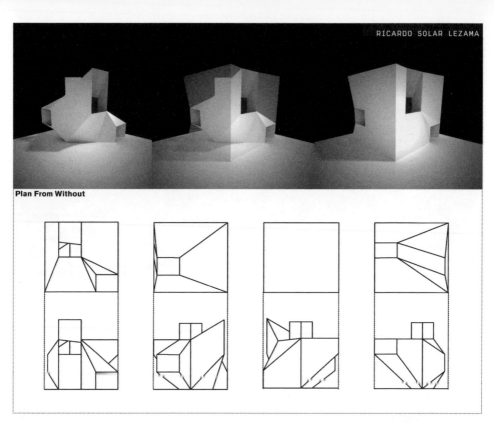

RICARDO SOLAR LEZAMA

Plan From Without

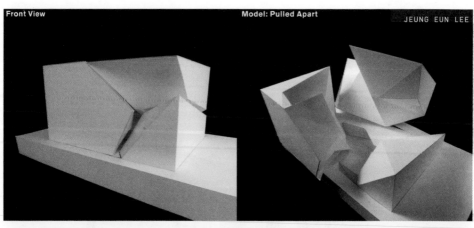

Front View　　　　　　　　　　　**Model: Pulled Apart**　　JEUNG EUN LEE

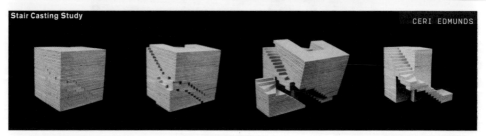

Stair Casting Study　　　　　　　　　　　　　　CERI EDMUNDS

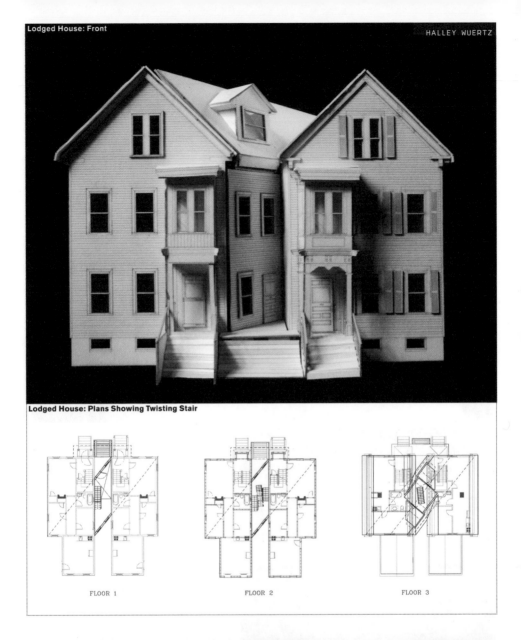

Lodged House: Front

HALLEY WUERTZ

Lodged House: Plans Showing Twisting Stair

FLOOR 1   FLOOR 2   FLOOR 3

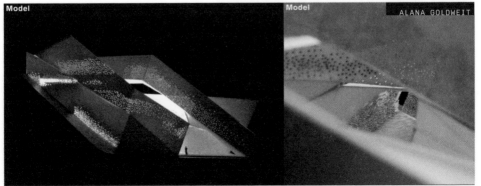

Model

Model

ALANA GOLDWEIT

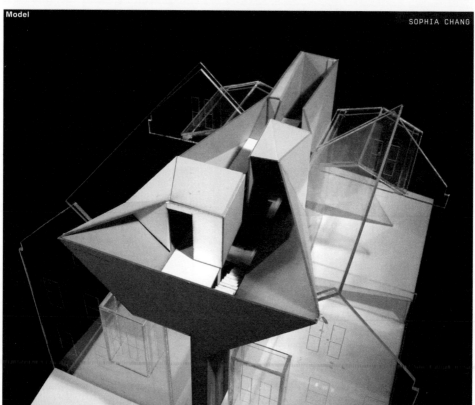

Model

Building Compression and Expansion

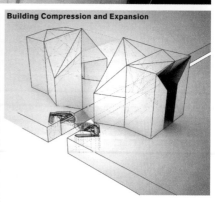

ANDREW PEDRON

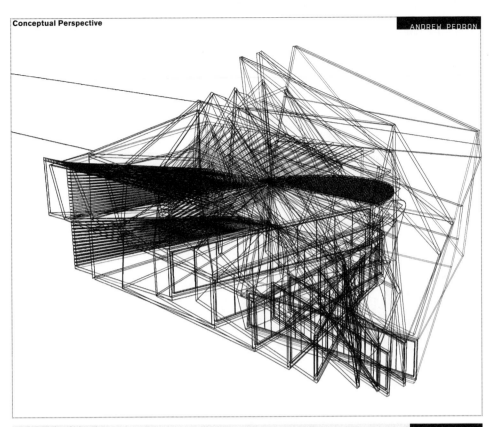

CHRISTIN TO

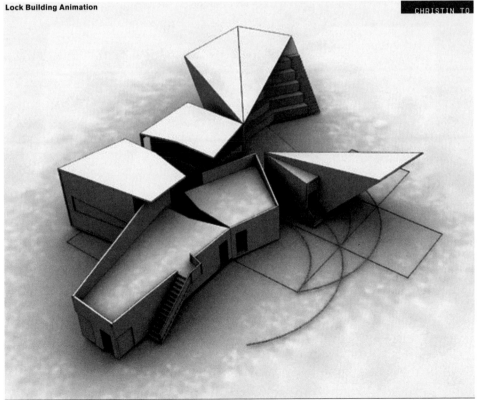

Movement

ALANA GOLDWEIT

- - - - - - - ARRIVAL
- - - - - - - DEPARTURE

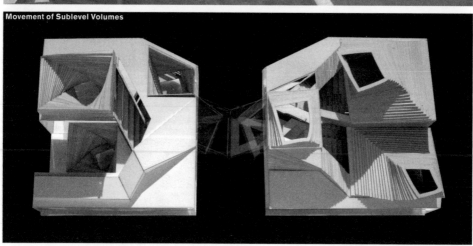

Movement of Sublevel Volumes

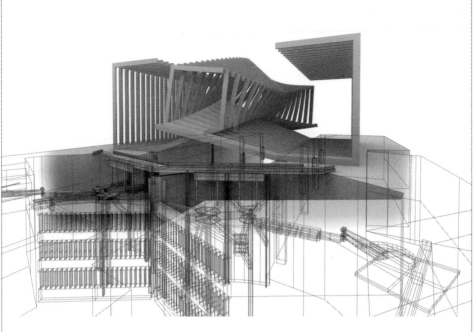

Sectional Movement

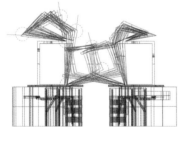

Model

LANDSCAPE ARCHITECTURE I

CORE   INSTRUCTORS:
MICHAEL BLIER, EMILY WAUGH, MARTHA SCHWARTZ   FALL 2009

The design studio is the fundamental component of education at the Graduate School of Design, and as such, is the primary locus for the integration of coursework in history, theory, technology, and representation. GSD 1111 is the first of four core design studios in the Department of Landscape Architecture. This first semester course is an introduction to both the traditions and the techniques of the discipline of landscape architecture. The studio curriculum focused on a profound engagement with the phenomena of site and the creation of meaning through form as the major generative forces of landscape design. Through the design process, the studio investigated the relationships between form and personal expression, between form and cultural ideas, between design intent and its expression in a particular medium, between design intent and a specific place, and between theory and practice.

Material Study: Dewey Square Park

EMILY GORDON

Somerville High School Montage

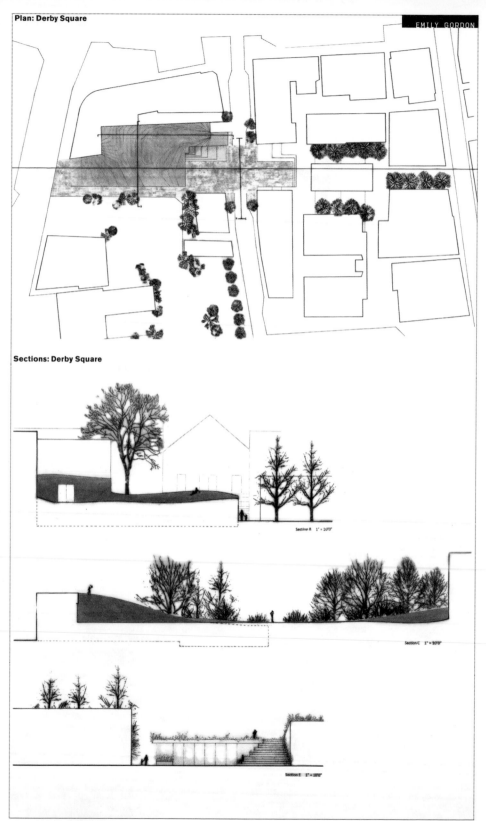

Plan: Derby Square

EMILY GORDON

Sections: Derby Square

Section B 1" = 10'0"

Section C 1" = 10'0"

Section E 1" = 10'0"

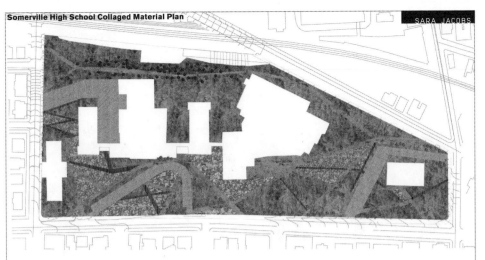

Somerville High School Collaged Material Plan

SARA JACOBS

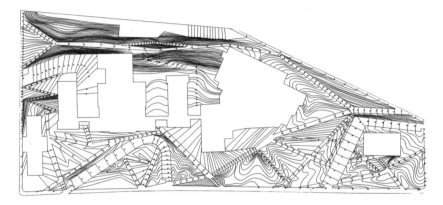

Somerville High School Grading Plan

Somerville High School Montage

Derby Square Montage

Derby Square Wind Diagrams

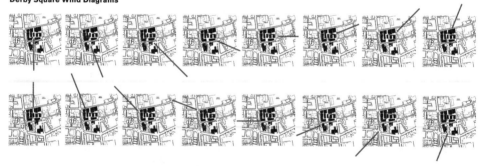

Somerville High School Montage

SARA JACOBS

Model

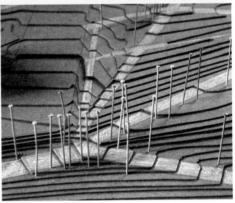

URBAN PLANNING I

CORE

INSTRUCTORS:
JUDITH GRANT LONG, KATHRYN MADDEN, KATHY SPIEGELMAN

FALL 2009

The first semester core studio of the Master of Urban Planning program introduces students to the fundamental knowledge and technical skills used by urban planners to create, research, analyze, and implement plans and projects for the built environment. The studio operates in conjunction with GSD 3329: Methods of Urban Planning, which introduces students to spatial analysis through GIS; visual representation techniques; projections and forecasts in plan-making, including how demographic, economic, and market forecasts inform land use and infrastructure needs assessments; how alternative land use scenarios are constructed, including approaches to allocating land use, estimating carrying capacity, and build-out analyses; and evaluation of land use impacts through fiscal, economic, social, environmental, and transportation frameworks.

The studio was organized into four parts, each representing a fundamental stage of the urban planning process.

Part 1 explores the importance of ideas and the process of generating ideas for urban planning.

Part 2 explores research skills used by urban planners to understand and analyze the built environment.

Part 3 explores the making of plans for the built environment at all scales.

Part 4 explores how to implement urban plans.

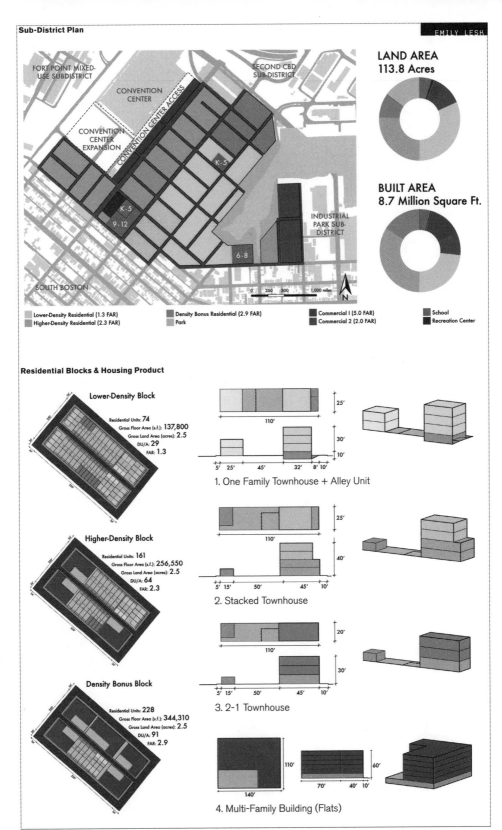

FORT POINT MIXED-USE SUBDISTRICT

CONVENTION CENTER

CONVENTION CENTER EXPANSION

CONVENTION CENTER ACCESS

SECOND CBD SUB-DISTRICT

K-5

K-5

9-12

INDUSTRIAL PARK SUB-DISTRICT

6-8

SOUTH BOSTON

0   250   500   1,000 miles

LAND AREA
113.8 Acres

BUILT AREA
8.7 Million Square Ft.

Lower-Density Residential (1.3 FAR)
Higher-Density Residential (2.3 FAR)
Density Bonus Residential (2.9 FAR)
Park
Commercial I (5.0 FAR)
Commercial 2 (2.0 FAR)
School
Recreation Center

Residential Blocks & Housing Product

Lower-Density Block

Residential Units: **74**
Gross Floor Area (s.f.): **137,800**
Gross Land Area (acres): **2.5**
DU/A: **29**
FAR: **1.3**

110'
25'
30'
10'
5' 25'   45'   32' 8' 10'

1. One Family Townhouse + Alley Unit

Higher-Density Block

Residential Units: **161**
Gross Floor Area (s.f.): **256,550**
Gross Land Area (acres): **2.5**
DU/A: **64**
FAR: **2.3**

110'
25'
40'
5' 15'   50'   45'   10'

2. Stacked Townhouse

Density Bonus Block

Residential Units: **228**
Gross Floor Area (s.f.): **344,310**
Gross Land Area (acres): **2.5**
DU/A: **91**
FAR: **2.9**

110'
20'
30'
5' 15'   50'   45'   10'

3. 2-1 Townhouse

110'
140'
70' 40' 10'
60'

4. Multi-Family Building (Flats)

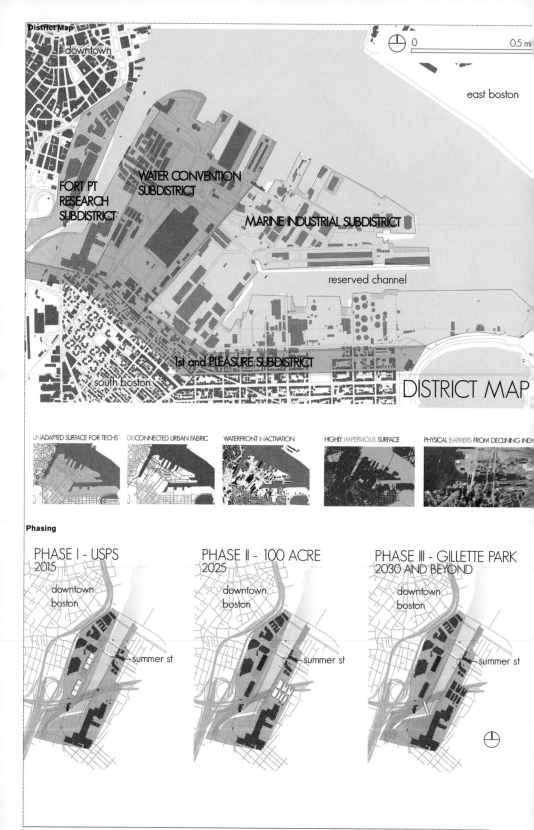

District Map

downtown

east boston

0   0.5 mi

FORT PT RESEARCH SUBDISTRICT

WATER CONVENTION SUBDISTRICT

MARINE INDUSTRIAL SUBDISTRICT

reserved channel

1st and PLEASURE SUBDISTRICT

south boston

DISTRICT MAP

UNADAPTED SURFACE FOR TECHS | DISCONNECTED URBAN FABRIC | WATERFRONT INACTIVATION | HIGHLY IMPERVIOUS SURFACE | PHYSICAL BARRIERS FROM DECLINING IND

Phasing

PHASE I - USPS
2015

downtown
boston

summer st

PHASE II - 100 ACRE
2025

downtown
boston

summer st

PHASE III - GILLETTE PARK
2030 AND BEYOND

downtown
boston

summer st

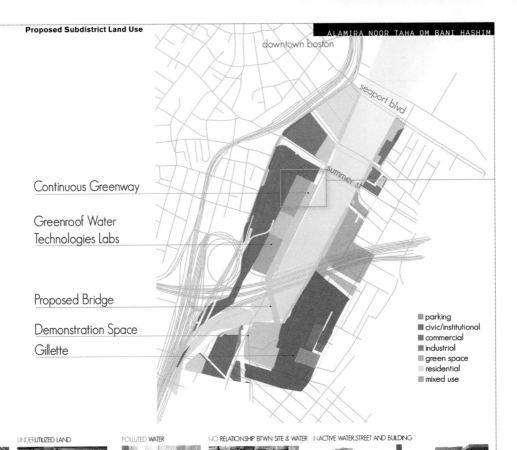

downtown boston

seaport blvd

summer st

Continuous Greenway

Greenroof Water
Technologies Labs

Proposed Bridge

Demonstration Space

Gillette

- parking
- civic/institutional
- commercial
- industrial
- green space
- residential
- mixed use

UNDERUTILIZED LAND · POLLUTED WATER · NO RELATIONSHIP BTWN SITE & WATER · INACTIVE WATER, STREET AND BUILDING

Perspective Drawing of Envisioned Waterfront

Ecological Edge: Restored Salt Marshes + Revamped Harbor Walk

Existing Conditions + Ecological Edge Proposal

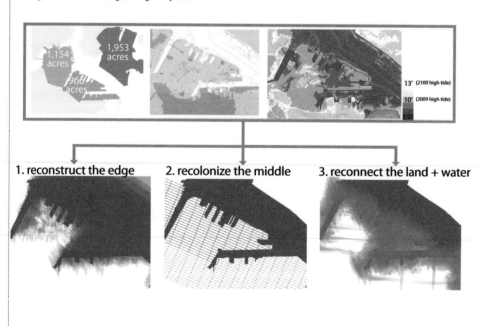

1,154 acres

1,953 acres

960 acres

13' (2100 high tide)

10' (2009 high tide)

1. reconstruct the edge

2. recolonize the middle

3. reconnect the land + water

Site Plan

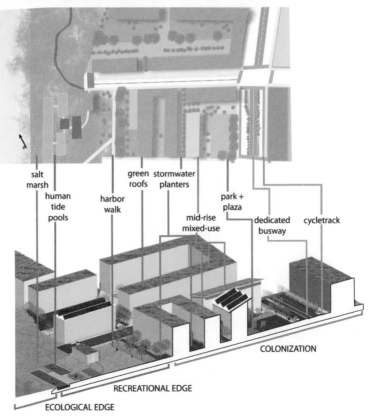

salt marsh

human tide pools

harbor walk

green roofs

stormwater planters

mid-rise mixed-use

park + plaza

dedicated busway

cycletrack

COLONIZATION

RECREATIONAL EDGE

ECOLOGICAL EDGE

From Infrastructure to Ecostructure: Core Parcels with Existing and Proposed Context

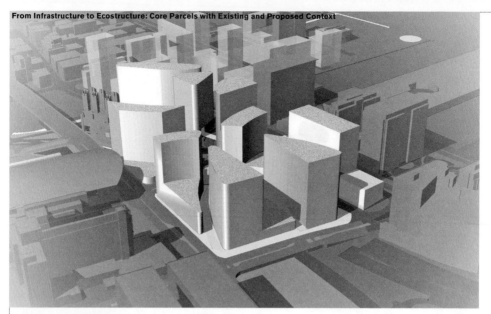

Phasing the Core Parcels

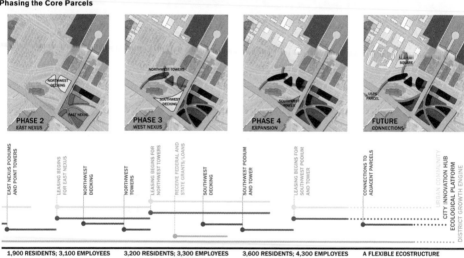

PHASE 2
EAST NEXUS

PHASE 3
WEST NEXUS

PHASE 4
EXPANSION

FUTURE
CONNECTIONS

KLARIHI SQUARE

USPS PARCEL

NORTHWEST DECKING

EAST NEXUS

NORTHWEST TOWERS

SOUTHWEST DECKING

SOUTHWEST TOWER

EAST NEXUS PODIUMS AND POINT TOWERS

LEASING BEGINS FOR EAST NEXUS

NORTHWEST DECKING

NORTHWEST TOWERS

LEASING BEGINS FOR NORTHWEST TOWERS

RECEIVE FEDERAL AND STATE GRANTS / LOANS

SOUTHWEST DECKING

SOUTHWEST PODIUM AND TOWER

LEASING BEGINS FOR SOUTHWEST PODIUM AND TOWER

CONNECTIONS TO ADJACENT PARCELS

URBAN COMMUNITY

CITY INNOVATION HUB

ECOLOGICAL PLATFORM

DISTRICT GROWTH ENGINE

1,900 RESIDENTS; 3,100 EMPLOYEES   3,200 RESIDENTS; 3,300 EMPLOYEES   3,600 RESIDENTS; 4,300 EMPLOYEES   A FLEXIBLE ECOSTRUCTURE

East Nexus

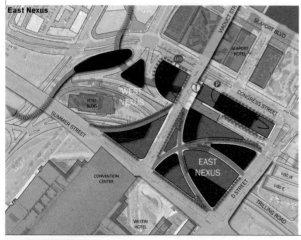

VIADUCT STR

SEAPORT BLVD

SEAPORT HOTEL

BLVD

CONGRESS STREET

VENT BLDG

WEST NEXUS

SUMMER STREET

EAST NEXUS

CONVENTION CENTER

D STREET

I-90 W

I-90 E

TRILLING ROAD

WESTIN HOTEL

Focusing on a Sectional Subdistrict

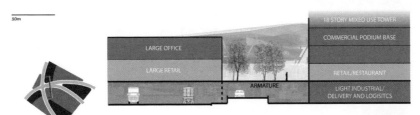

ARMATURE

LARGE OFFICE

LARGE RETAIL

ARMATURE

18 STORY MIXED USE TOWER

COMMERCIAL PODIUM BASE

RETAIL/RESTAURANT

LIGHT INDUSTRIAL/
DELIVERY AND LOGISITCS

TRILLING ROAD   D STREET OFF-RAMP

AIRPORT TUNNEL
APPROACH

PROMENADE

18 STORY MIXED USE TOWER

COMMERCIAL PODIUM BASE

RESTAURANT/RETAIL

PROMENADE

SUMMER ROAD   RAIL   TRILLING ROAD   RAMP / VENT BUILDING

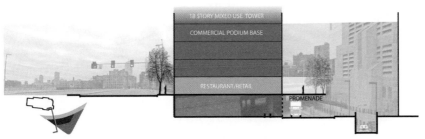

ARCADE

18 STORY MIXED USE TOWER

RESTAURANT

RETAIL

LOBBY

ARCADE

HOTEL DROP-OFF   CONGRESS STREET   GALE PROPERTIES PARCELS

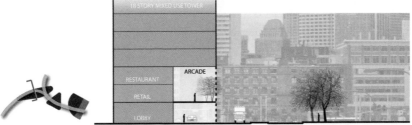

HARVARD GSD SYMPOSIA ON ARCHITECTURE: THE RETURN OF NATURE

SYMPOSIUM | PRESTON SCOTT COHEN | INTRODUCTORY REMARKS

SPEAKERS:
SYLVIA LAVIN, ROBERT LEVIT, FARSHID MOUSSAVI, BARRY BERGDOL, K. MICHAEL HAYS, DIANE LEWIS, MARK JARZOMBEK, ANDREW PAYNE, FRANCOIS ROCHE, ELIZABETH DILLER, ANTOINE PICON, PETER EISENMAN, JORGE SILVETTI, SARAH WHITING

In one reading, the nature of Architecture, a title suggested to me by Jorge Silvetti, suggests the essence of architecture —or the natural within it, whether it be the forces of gravity or the temperature of the air that whirls around it. Structure could be the nature of architecture since it manifests forces of gravity. On the other hand, since we know that Jorge would not ascribe to the naturalization of architecture, we could have called tonight's event "the return of the unnatural," and Peter suggested that to me after I had already named it—or the return of architecture, which is to say, artifice, never natural. And while no one would say that ecology is anything other than unnatural first and foremost, the unnaturalness of architecture is a very different thing, and this I believe will be something we cannot avoid talking about tonight.

Clearly architecture has fought nature but it has aligned with nature too, by abstracting it according to an idea, a system or form. The green ideology, on the other hand, more limitedly calls forth, in its most positivistic manifestations, functional parameters unrelated to architecture as artifice. With the new sustainable functionalism, artifice can only be accepted when it too becomes a commodity function, and yet, this must be renounced.

If the ascendency of sustainability, and positivistic, scientistic, vitalist, and organicist tendencies replace artifice and representation, where does this put architecture?

Spring 2010
The Harvard GSD Symposia on Architecture

The Return of Nature

February 24
**The Apparatus
of Sustainability**
Mark Jarzombek
Andrew Payne
François Roche

March 31
**The Nature of
Information**
Elizabeth Diller
Antoine Picon

April 13
**The Nature of
Architecture**
Peter Eisenman
Jorge Silvetti
Sarah Whiting

Piper Auditorium   6:30 - 8:00
Graduate School of Design
Harvard University

Co-convened by
Preston Scott Cohen
Erika Naginski

François Roche/R&Sie(n), Paris, 2006

I'll refrain from a frontal assault, but just give a little tap: the
green is too often an ideological cover for the domination it
perpetrates but claims to subvert. In the dream of totalization
in which architecture, landscape and urban planning are
unified, what happens to the unnatural nature of architecture?
It is a difficult question because architecture by its nature
is incompatible with this functionalized unity since it always
stands apart from it.

Perhaps then we could ask the question from a different
position. What would happen if architecture took over
everything? If it grew like weeds. Nothing regulating its
bestial ambitions. It might turn out that we've seen this before
in the poignant allegory of Piranesi Campo Marzio, where the
drive to take over everything turns the city into a monstrosity.
Here, and today once more, in order to set itself apart again,
architecture will have to reinvent itself.

Fall 2009
The Harvard Symposia on Architecture

The Return of Nature

September 16
**Organicism Contra
Ornament**
Sylvia Lavin
Robert Levit
Farshid Moussavi

October 7
**The Limits of
Sustainability**
Elizabeth Diller
Mark Jarzombek
Andrew Payne

November 17
The Sublime Plan
Barry Bergdoll
K. Michael Hays
Diane Lewis

Piper Auditorium 6:30 - 8:00
Graduate School of Design
Harvard University

Co-convened by
Preston Scott Cohen
Erika Naginski

Spring 2010
The Harvard GSD Symposia on Architecture

The Return of Nature

February 24
**The Apparatus
of Sustainability**
Mark AJarzombek
Andrew Payne
François Roche

March 31
**The Nature of
Information**
Elizabeth Diller
Antoine Picon

April 13
**The Nature of
Architecture**
Peter Eisenman
Jorge Silvetti
Sarah Whiting

Piper Auditorium 6:30 - 8:00
Graduate School of Design
Harvard University

Co-convened by
Preston Scott Cohen
Erika Naginski

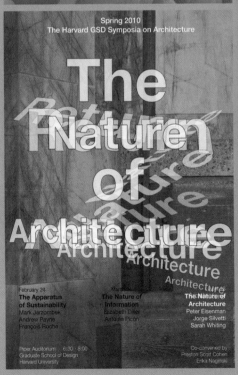

Spring 2010
The Harvard GSD Symposia on Architecture

The Nature of Architecture

February 24
**The Apparatus
of Sustainability**
Mark Jarzombek
Andrew Payne
François Roche

March 31
**The Nature of
Information**
Elizabeth Diller
Antoine Picon

**The Nature of
Architecture**
Peter Eisenman
Jorge Silvetti
Sarah Whiting

Piper Auditorium 6:30 - 8:00
Graduate School of Design
Harvard University

Co-convened by
Preston Scott Cohen
Erika Naginski

Fall 2009
The Harvard Symposia on Architecture

The Return of Nature

September 16
**Organicism Contra
Ornament**
Sylvia Lavin
Robert Levit
Farshid Moussavi

October 7
**The Limits of
Sustainability**
Elizabeth Diller
Mark Jarzombek
Andrew Payne

November 17
The Sublime Plan
Barry Bergdoll
K. Michael Hays
Diane Lewis

Piper Auditorium 6:30 - 8:00
Graduate School of Design
Harvard University

Co-convened by
Preston Scott Cohen
Erika Naginski

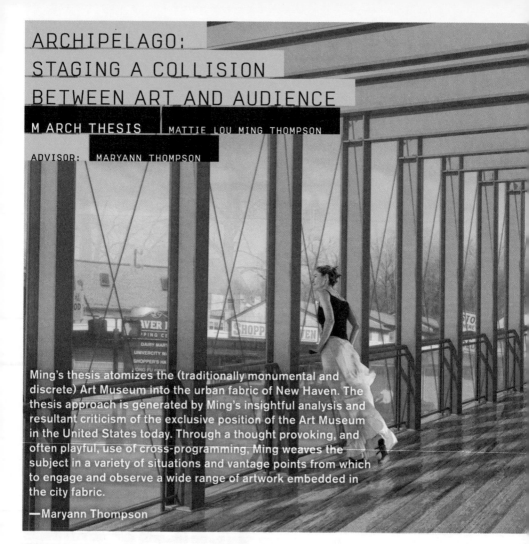

ARCHIPELAGO: STAGING A COLLISION BETWEEN ART AND AUDIENCE

M ARCH THESIS | MATTIE LOU MING THOMPSON

ADVISOR: MARYANN THOMPSON

Ming's thesis atomizes the (traditionally monumental and discrete) Art Museum into the urban fabric of New Haven. The thesis approach is generated by Ming's insightful analysis and resultant criticism of the exclusive position of the Art Museum in the United States today. Through a thought provoking, and often playful, use of cross-programming, Ming weaves the subject in a variety of situations and vantage points from which to engage and observe a wide range of artwork embedded in the city fabric.

—Maryann Thompson

This thesis project attempts to expand access to the art museum by re-envisioning the museum experience at the scale of the city, the building, and the gallery. The proposed museum is urbanistically engaged, anti-monumental, and encourages new ways of looking at art within the gallery space. The archipelago draws upon architectural characteristics that will counter the traditional continental paradigm with dispersal, porosity, and programmatic juxtaposition. The museum is fragmented, exploded into a set of related pieces that are sited within the communities it seeks to serve. Each site offers a distinct contextual framework corresponding to an art typology, allowing each unit to explore a specific spatial configuration suited to each type. The museum is opportunistic, squeezing itself into the abandoned and unnoticed spaces of the city, drawing from the vast and rarely exhibited resources of existing museums, and working to commission its own artwork. The project sets out to create strategic collisions between art and the audience, opening a dialogue between art and community. The art experience is taken out of the generic spaces of the museum, and made truly contingent, shaped by its context. The museum is not simply reflective of its culture, but generative, acting as a site for new and unexpected interpretations and encounters.

Site A: Model

Thesis Instigate Evolution

Site B: The Hill

Site B: Model

Site C: Model

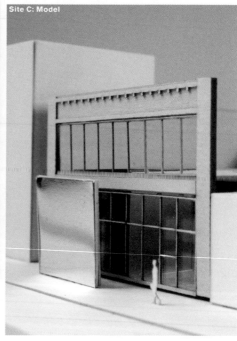

Site C: Fair Haven

Site D: Sculpture in the Playground

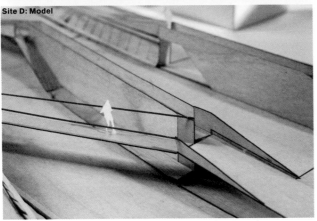
Site D: Model

Site C: Video Art in the Laundromat

FLAT TO FORM: DESIGN AND MANUFACTURE OF COMPOSITE SHELLS WITHOUT MOLDS

MDESS THESIS | MATAN MAYER

ADVISORS: MARTIN BECHTHOLD, MARIANA IBANEZ

While emergent production technologies in architecture allow greater precision in multiple materials, they do very little to reduce manufacturing-associated waste in common processes, such as custom mold-making. This thesis looked into developing a zero-waste production method for free-form composite building envelopes, using readily available fabrication tools, such as a six axis water jet cutter as well as computational processing. The computational procedure developed as part of the thesis essentially takes a given form, rationalizes it into a series of planar panels, populates it with an interlocking teeth system which works much like a 3D zipper, unrolls it into a flat sheet, and produces a machine code for a robotic water jet cutter. Additionally, this production method allows the user to vary the manufactured panel's porosity to correspond with structural requirements, such as shear stress. This is achieved through a finite element analysis of the panel, which in turn produces a pattern of cavities in varying sizes. The research received the 2010 Peter Rice Prize for innovation in architecture and structural design.

Light Penetration

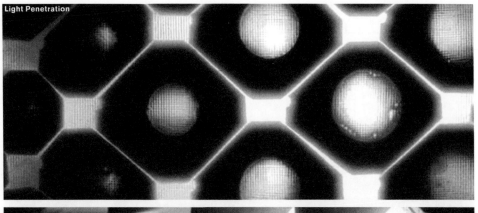

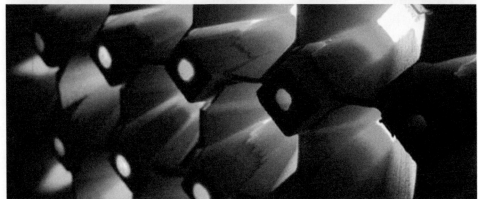

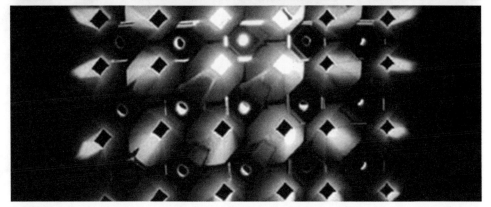

Assembled Panel

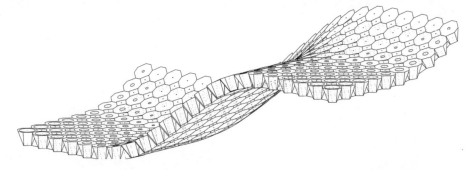

Thesis Instigate Evolution

WATER CITY HAMBURG - THE MISSING LINK

OPTION STUDIO   HENRI BAVA

Hamburg is a booming European metropolis and the Wilhelmsburg Island, which lies between two major branches of the River Elbe, represents the city's key development area for the future. The current urban development program "leap over the Elbe" underlines the city's ambition to integrate this peripheral and neglected area into the city structure. The International Building Exhibition, IBA, will be held at the center of the Wilhelmsburg Island in 2013, and at the same time it will host the International Garden Show.

These two major events represent the first phase of a long-term urban construction process for the Wilhelmsburg Island. Consequently, the center strip of the island will be defined as a system of parks running, from Hamburg harbor in the North, to the rural areas in the South, crossing and assimilating parts of existing structures.

The option studio investigated the landscape potential of this site, which covers an area of 40 hectares. Students were expected to develop the "missing link" in this system of parks and to establish a new residential area. Water in its various forms is the leitmotif for the design. The option studio included an optional site visit to Wilhelmsburg Island, and to the ongoing project of HafenCity, which is one of the largest inner city rebuilding projects in Europe.

View Along Top of Linear Park

EMILY BONIFACI

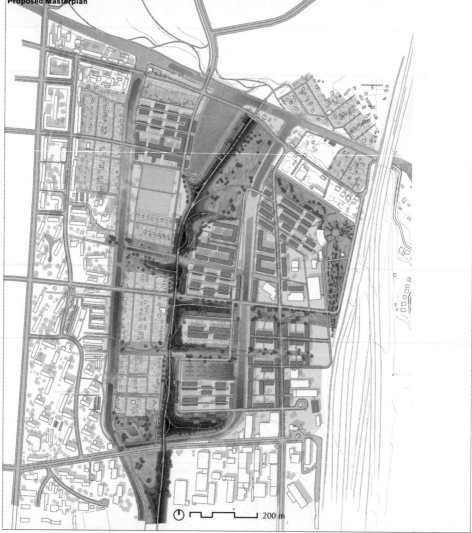

Proposed Masterplan

200 m

Wilhelmsburg Skyline

IZABELA RIANO

Building Typology

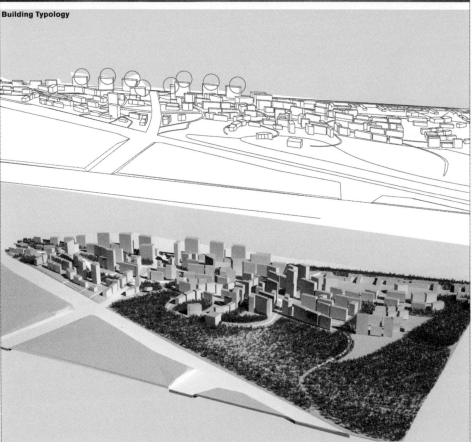

Option Studio Instigate Evolution

Residential Axis: Low-Density Residential Area

Masterplan

veddel station area
veddel station plaza
stairs
lower shopping street
inner street

recreational marsh

waterfront park
water lock

dijk entrance
canal walk
pier
promenade on the dijk

existing forest

pocket park

restaurant

low-density residential area
bikepath on the ground

watermeadow

pedestrian pathway
container park

baumanlage
extend existing allee
end station
park under the trees

bunker

social housings
primary canal
community gardens

industrial area
secondary canal wetland

elevated bikepath

wilhelmsburg station area
sports fields
campus exstention
staatliche schule gesundheitspflege

TBA harbor

Circuit Trail: Perspective + Section

MAKI SHINDO

promenade from weddel station   barburger chaussee   klutjenfelder hauptdeich   platform on the river   pier extension to the north

circuit trail E-W sections
(on the dijk)

Residential Axis: Container Park

THE NEW GATE: PUBLIC SPACE, INFRASTRUCTURE AND THE RE-ORIENTATION OF HISTORIC ISTANBUL

OPTION STUDIO | HASHIM SARKIS

Over the past four decades, the city of Istanbul has grown away from the congestion of its historic center towards its vast metropolitan fringes on both sides of the Bosphorus supported by an extensive network of roads, bridges, and public transportation. This condition is bound to radically change in 2011, when the Marmaray project, a new underwater train-line linking the two sides of the Bosphorus, will be completed. This line will bring more than one million passengers a day into the historic city. Yenikapi (Turkish for "new gate"), an existing station at the intersection of ferry and metro lines right next to the Roman wall of the historic city, will be enlarged to serve as main station for the Marmaray. From Yenikapi, commuters will work their way from the inner city out.

Yenikapi:

The new geographic repositioning of the historic city will require enhancing and reorienting its public spaces. The site of Yenikapi is already highly urbanized. It is further challenged by archaeological findings of a Byzantine harbor (probably destroyed by an earthquake), the city's disaster relief program (primarily in face of earthquakes), and the sectional relations among the different parts of the site add to the challenges of building a station and the public spaces required for its proper functioning. The interstitial spaces between the different modes of transportation will require a clearer connection logic as this site is readied to become literally the new gate for the one million commuters.

The studio, offered in collaboration with Bilgi University in Istanbul, explored the intersection of these different infrastructural components in the historic city around the program of a new station. Students proposed design solutions for this station and its different components, including entry points and public spaces, retail activity, a disaster relief center, and bridges and passages. They were encouraged to push the relationship between urban development and public space towards a new conception of the role of infrastructure in reorienting the city.

Yenikapi Station in Cross Section

LORETA CASTRO REGUERA MANCERA

Model

Site Plan

Eye Level View: Rest Area

CHUNG WHAN PARK

Model

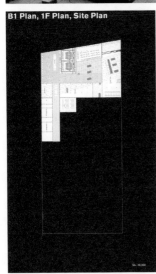
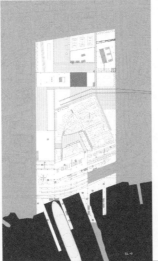

B1 Plan, 1F Plan, Site Plan

Option Studio Instigate Evolution

BORROWING NATURE'S BLUEPRINTS: BIOMIMICRY AND THE ART OF WELL-ADAPTED DESIGN

HOK/BILL VALENTINE LECTURE

JANINE BENYUS   DECEMBER 1, 2009. EXCERPT

When I say "biomimicry," I'm not talking about putting
pictures of leaves on wallpaper. I'm talking about function.
Biomimicry is a conscious emulation, and it's at three levels.
It's mimicking form or shape. Life uses shape for function.
And it's also mimicking process, which is everything from
mimicking photosynthesis to mimicking natural selection itself
as an optimizing program in things like genetic algorithms.
The third level is mimicking at the ecosystem level.

My question is, "What if our cities performed as well as natural ecosystems,
and what is it going to take for us to
be part of that long line of species that
have figured out a system that is sustainable for all?"

"How do they cache water? How do they build? What
materials do they use to build? How do they cool? How do
they heat themselves?" We ask those questions, and it's
not metaphorical. We're actually looking for design insights.
We're looking for principles.

Take, for example, an organism called brittle star. Its skeleton
is also a series of lenses to let light in, which Lucent
Technology at Bell Labs were very interested in because
those calcite lenses are incredibly good fine focus lenses.
It's a single crystal of calcite, and yet, there is very, very little
distortion in that lens. What's even more interesting is that
it self-assembles out of seawater, so it's not just an amazing
form, but the process is also amazing.

Or the venus sea basket. It's the skeleton of a sea sponge
that has filaments that are wave guides. They're like our fiber
optics. They work as well as our fiber optics, but what's
interesting about them is that you can tie them in a knot. And
again, self-assembled. They're basically a silicate. It's glass.
Self-assembled out of sea water, and yet, in a very incredible
architecture that can act as a wave guide, but with a flexibility

that we don't yet have. So imagine if you were able to spec fiber optic sun tubes that would be able to bend around corners without breaking. It would be a very, very different situation than what we currently have.

So what can buildings learn from nature?

What if you had to ask your building skin to be as good as a tree? I mean, what would it really look like in terms of gathering water, gathering its own sunlight, and distributing its own water? I mean, think of all the things a tree can do.

What about adaptive buildings where things like louvers can open and close and often use motors and pulleys and cables to make them move? Life doesn't do that. A flower doesn't have a pulley or a motor telling it to close its petals when it's nighttime.

Life literally created the lushness that we now enjoy over 3,800,000,000 years, and my sense is that we can figure out how to continue that tradition, but first we've got to figure out how to create conditions conducive to life, because life is at the center of every decision that's made in organisms.

And even the natural selection process, as agnostic as it is, rewards that which is good for life over the long-haul. It's not just about the technologies.

There's a thing that happens with biomimicry. It's an emotion that's a lot more powerful than the guilt that we often have now; it's respect.

We are so young as a species on this earth. We really are like toddlers with matches. But we're not aliens. We sprang from this earth. We belong here. We're a biological organism, and we belong here. Natural selection will teach us manners.

DEREK CHAN

Describe Identity

The following selections illustrate the ability of the built environment to carry the identity of an individual, a place, or a society. Design can give value through differentiation, solidify through reinforcement, alter perception through change, and even define who we are by how we relate to it.

ERRATICS:
A GENEALOGY OF ROCK LANDSCAPE
FEATURING THE WORK OF
CLAUDE CORMIER ARCHITECTES
PAYSAGISTES

EXHIBITION   CLAUDE CORMIER ARCHITECTES PAYSAGISTES

Erratics proposes a speculative genealogy of rock-based landscape architecture, featuring work associated with Harvard University, the Graduate School of Design, and the Department of Landscape Architecture. This array of sites, scales, and approaches is paired with a presentation of projects by Montreal-based Claude Cormier (MDesS '94), an emerging international voice and principal of Claude Cormier Architectes Paysagistes, one of Canada's leading landscape architecture firms. Sugar Beach, Cormier's recent public landscape on the Toronto waterfront, is the point of connection for these two explorations; this project exemplifies landscape architecture's longstanding fascination with erratics—rocks deposited by glacial movements—and the opportunities for invention that they inspire.

On view are significant precursors to Sugar Beach, including SWA's (Peter Walker) Tanner Fountain on the Harvard Campus (1985); the granite outcropping in Martha Schwartz, Ken Smith, and David Meyer's Yorkville Park in Toronto (1994); Michael Van Valkenburgh Associates' Teardrop Park in New York City (2004); and Workshop: Ken Smith Landscape Architect's MoMA Roof Garden in New York City (2005). Sugar Beach is the latest of seventeen landscapes designed by CCAP over the past decade—projects animated by their use of color, camouflage, and games of visual perception.

With this juxtaposition of modes of operation within landscape architecture, around a common theme, Erratics emphasizes the complex and sometimes contradictory affinities and influences associated with disciplinary and professional cultures, while also revealing the internal consistency and explicit methodological concerns of the designer as autonomous agent.

Describe Identity **Exhibition**

Cormier's work reminds us of the centrality of the viewing subject in the production of landscape. In fact, landscape intervenes between us and the world, and in so doing, produces the world for us.

—Charles Waldheim

"Colombia is a little different from the rest of Latin America because we do not have a strong heritage of architecture like Brazil, or Argentina, or even Chile, so I don't believe we have a really 'Colombian' architecture. We have lots of them because our landscape and the people are very diverse. Even the vernacular architecture inside our country is diverse, so sometimes it looks like a lot of countries inside one."

"We believe that putting things out of context is a powerful tool for design. We take a lot of trips and we find a lot of different landscapes on our travels. We like to decontextualize them to insert them artificially into other projects to make a new kind of landscape, or a new place. It becomes a collage of all the other landscapes that we keep collecting as we travel around the world."

EPHEMERAL CROSSROADS.
THE NATIONAL OGALLALA AQUIFER TRAIL:
AN INDEX // AN IMPETUS

MLA THESIS | ERIK PRINCE

ADVISORS: CHRIS REED, CHARLES WALDHEIM

The enormous Ogallala Aquifer is one of the largest aquifers in the world. It consists of relatively shallow groundwater trapped below the High Plains, consisting of eight western states across 174,000 square miles of fertile but otherwise dry plains farmland. The Ogallala Aquifer has transformed the High Plains region from Dust Bowl to Bread Basket at the flip of a switch. The aquifer is a relict deposit in a semi-arid climate subject to extreme droughts and regularly receives no more than an inch of recharge each year, yet it is extracted to a net deficit of nearly twelve billion gallons of water a day to support 20 billion dollars in food and fiber annually. The region's vitality is dependent on the aquifer and the aquifer's exhaustion puts it at a "risk of overall regional collapse." The Ogallala Aquifer region is ripe with tension between necessary economic growth and critical resource conservation.

Ephemeral Crossroads acknowledges the Ogallala as a threatened national natural resource and the paramount importance to the landscape and the culture that relies on it. Since the region is more than 90 percent privately owned with diverse state and local ownership of the aquifer, a singular engineered or preservation-based regional master plan to "save" the aquifer and sustain the region is wrought with problems. Ephemeral Crossroads moves beyond a singular prescriptive master plan and proposes a juncture for design initially to index and appreciate the typically invisible aquifer to local communities, the region, nation and world. It further proposes to foster a stewardship of the region, its energy producing capabilities, and the aquifer through a built public network of multi-faceted and multi-functional regional trails/roads that intersect and transform with the local conditions to provide an infrastructural framework to crystallize resources and community, and provide the impetus for social, ecological, and functional resiliency in the landscape.

Concept Diagram

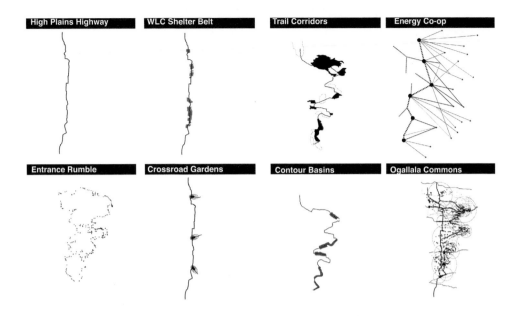

| High Plains Highway | WLC Shelter Belt | Trail Corridors | Energy Co-op |
| Entrance Rumble | Crossroad Gardens | Contour Basins | Ogallala Commons |

Crossroad Garden Aerial Perspective

Thesis Describe Identity

Grain Elevator Index

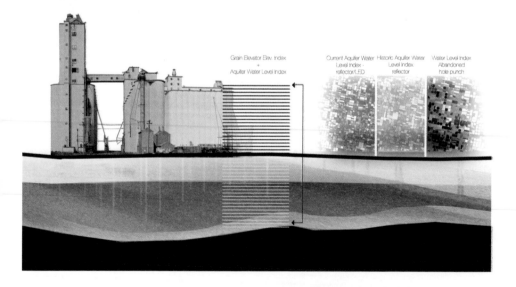

Grain Elevator Elev. Index
+
Aquifer Water Level Index

Current Aquifer Water Level Index - reflector/LED

Historic Aquifer Water Level Index reflector

Water Level Index Abandoned hole punch

Crossroad Garden Perspective

WLC Shelter Belt

shelter belt aerial [near lubbock tx]
existing condition [2006]

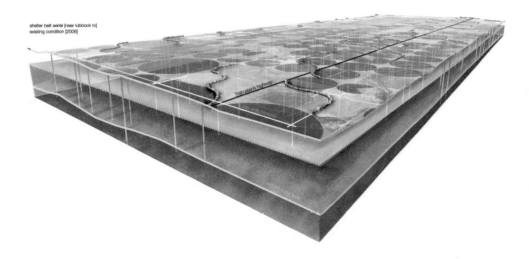

Thesis Describe Identity

CONTINUITY, INTEGRATION, INTEGRITY

OPTION STUDIO | YVONNE FARRELL, SHELLEY MCNAMARA

It takes deep thought to weave into a culture. As architects, we love the opportunity to spend time evaluating a new place, its territory, its form, its formation, its culture, colors, texture, scale, and character.

When we see images of cities destroyed, obliterated, we realize how buildings 'hold' culture and civilization. Buildings are the mirrors of values. They tell the story of our lives in built form. With globalization, architecture's role to 'hold' culture is even more critical. We walk through and feel places with our whole bodies with all our senses, not just with our eyes or with our minds. We are fully involved in the experience—this is what makes us human. When architecture is referred to as the mother of the arts, it is describing the all-encompassing nature of building, which actually envelops you, doing so over time, each day, throughout the seasons. Architecture is a shield and a protector of our humanity. As more of the natural world disappears, what we do as architects in making this new landscape of buildings has deep, societal repercussions.

The location for this project was in the university city of Toulouse, France, which pre-dates the Romans. It has integrated into its built form layers of expressions over centuries of continuity. A student site visit to Toulouse studied its nature and character, and enabled students to experience and record it both scientifically and emotionally. Each student documented and interpreted specific Elements of Toulouse as an integral part of their design methodology.

Individual student design work was carried out concurrently at a range of scales, allowing students to explore ways of simultaneously creating space and making buildings.

Parallel with the design of the building project, students performed in-depth case studies to rediscover the integrity of buildings as intellectual and physical architectural experiments, with specific emphasis on the impact on space of context, use, structure, and the physicality of materials.

School of Architecture along the Garonne River

HAVANA IN OUR TIME: DEVELOPING URBAN DESIGN AND PLANNING STRATEGIES FOR CHANGE

OPTION STUDIO   LELAND COTT

Havana, Cuba, once known as the Pearl of the Antilles, is facing unprecedented pressure for change from increasing tourism, foreign economic interests and the likelihood of an end to the U.S. embargo. How the Cuban Government might balance the pressures of its growing tourist industry and expanding real estate development interest from abroad against the preservation of Havana's historic urban fabric formed the basis of this semester's challenge. This studio studied Havana's physical environment and proposed planning guidelines and urban design strategies to address sensitive growth issues. New development in Havana must be viable economically and socially but it must also be sustainable and respectful of the city's unique natural and built environment.

Students studied Havana's 450-year history as a planned city and the forces of change that threaten it. They proposed "protective" urban design and planning measures followed by a series of design case studies. Attention was focused on four districts of the city: the harbor customs house district and its outdated cruise ship facilities; the Malecon, Havana's historic seaside boulevard: La Rampa, Havana's 1950's pre-revolution modern casino and nightclub district; and the Paseo del Prado, Havana's most beautiful street redesigned early in the twentieth century by noted landscape architect Jean-Claude Nicolas Forrestier.

The future of Havana is of critical interest to Cuban planners, architects and public officials who are increasingly concerned about the negative effects of unplanned or explosive growth on the city's fragile environment. The results of this studio's work were published and distributed in Havana.

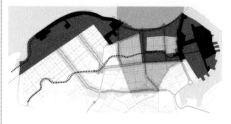

CENTRO HABANA
- Currently planned tourist zones
- Actual tourist centers
- •••• Proposed small-scale tourism development corridors
- Vulnerable zones

SCENARIO 1

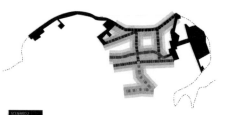

SCENARIO 2

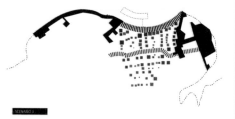

SCENARIO 3

Development Variations: Survey Patterns

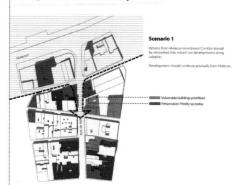

Scenario 1

Returns from Malecon Investment Corridor should be reinvested into mixed-use developments along cidzadas.

Development should continue gradually from Malecon.

- Vulnerable buildings prioritized
- Preservation Priority secondary

Scenario 2

Priority properties must be identified.

1. Land and buildings along the Malecon can be made available for lease.
2. Vulnerable structures
3. Historic buildings

Vacant lots outside the Malecon are lowest priority

- Malecon Lease Corridor
- Vulnerable buildings priority
- Historic buildings

Scenario 2

Returns from lease sales are to be put into an entrepreneurial fund. Funds are to be distributed on a competitive basis to Centro Habana residents towards the creation of small business and renovations.

Basically an entrepreneurial microbrigade.

- Entrepreneurial zones

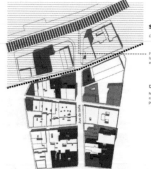

Scenario 3

Owners receive freehold status.

Publically owned land along the Malecon is either sold or leased at low rates and linked to improvements to the Malecon.

- Affordable Rental Development

Revenues from land sales fund early housing developments through public-private partnerships

Facade Interior

Option Studio Describe Identity

COMPLETE VOIDS

M ARCH THESIS NATHAN FASH

ADVISOR: PETER ROWE

Nathan's thesis raised the intriguing although widely present issue of how sites within a city might be appropriated temporarily for public use on the way to becoming more permanently transformed. In addressing this issue, he playfully yet precisely examined the implications of different durations of temporality in various urban conditions through three well-wrought design proposals.

—Peter Rowe

Despite the proclaimed decline of the public sphere with the rise of privatization and electronic media, the need for physical city spaces in which to gather, protest, shop, recreate, relax, experience difference, and to develop one's identity remains distinctly present today. Increased awareness of environmental degradation and climate change further strengthens the case for the economies of dense cities. The urgency of improving livability in cities underlines in turn the reciprocity between public space and quality of life.

Designers working in cities should do more to capitalize on public space as a resource to generate real value for public and private land holders, as well as the city and its population at large. A flexible attitude toward temporality, where a project might last as little as a few months, opens up a more fruitful range of possibilities for client and designer than the typical all-or-nothing approach. The projected permanence of a proposal has a ripple effect on design considerations such as the selection of materials, the complexity of construction, and programmatic possibilities, among others. This thesis takes on three different urban voids and proposes three different temporally based projects that demonstrate the importance and value of solutions of variable permanence that are driven by public space ideas.

Expectations for and uses of urban public space emerge out of a complex intersection of culture, politics, economics, climate, history, and geography, and are variable from one city to the next. By selecting three sites within Boston, a city that is imminently observable and urbanistically rich, the thesis emphasizes the influence of contextual contingencies. Taken together, the three proposals are an argument in favor of site-sensitive place making at the intersection of architecture, landscape, and urban design, in an era when architects are often called upon to design iconic object buildings alone. The collection of projects represents a search for responsive architectural forms that serve a social purpose beyond visual effect and image-making, a quest for public space that spurs participation.

Thesis Describe Identity

Model: Extreme Filene's

Model: Berklee Beach

Describe Identity **Thesis**

Model: Vertical Garden

IN DEFENSE OF "NATURAL SCENERY": FREDERICK LAW OLMSTED'S DISCURSIVE IDEOLOGY OF PRESERVATIONISM IN THE "PRELIMINARY REPORT UPON THE YOSEMITE VALLEY AND MARIPOSA BIG TREE GROVE"

MDESS THESIS   MEREDITH GAGLIO

ADVISOR: ANTOINE PICON

Meredith offers an incisive take into the origins of the American preservationist movement. Olmsted's "Preliminary Report upon the Yosemite Valley" is studied in depth to reveal the complex alliance between science, politics, and aesthetics that characterizes early preservationist concerns.

—Antoine Picon

Frederick Law Olmsted's "Preliminary Report upon the Yosemite and Big Tree Grove" (1865), though suppressed shortly after his departure from California, was a compendium of the Yosemite, reflective not only of his own diverse notions but also of the mid-nineteenth century environmental zeitgeist and the patriotic significance of the region as he experienced them. This thesis deliberately dissects Olmsted's Report in order to discover the preservationist inspirations and aspirations that drove his work in the Yosemite Valley from 1864 to 1865, and, through this investigation, to reflect upon the collision of architectural discourse, method, and practice with the concept of nature and environment in the mid-nineteenth century.

Image Sources: John Muir, The Yosemite, New York: The Century Co., 1912; *Hutchings' California Magazine* 4, no. 6 (December 1859); National Park Service, Frederick Law Olmsted National Historic Site, Brookline, Massachusetts.

Frederick Law Olmsted, c. 1860

General View of the Yosemite Valley, 1859

INSTRUCTORS: MICHAEL MEREDITH, DANIELLE ETZLER, ERIC HÖWELER,
CORE   MARIANA IBANEZ, THOMAS SCHROEPFER, CAMERON WU   SPRING 2010

The second of a four-semester sequence of design studios continues examination of the issues raised in the first semester and begins investigation of more complex issues related to building fabric.

ASSIGNMENT 1, ROOM: MODULE, FIGURE, WEIGHT

Task: Typically we think of the systemic organization as weightless networks, non-figural fields constructed from parts that form a diffuse whole. In this assignment we developed a systemic aggregation technique to produce a specific figure related to its own construction and occupation/use.

ASSIGNMENT 2: DISCRETE SERIALITY, SET THEORY

Task: Design an integrated system of modules—facade, book stacks, and reading carrels. There are three material systems that operate at different proportional scales from the building scale to the intimate body furniture scale. Students integrated these different systems of repetition as a single set with three coherent subsets of material and organizational logic. Like the previous assignment, this task was only a fragment of a building: the previous assignment was a single room, this was a thick cellular wall made of a series of rooms.

ASSIGNMENT 3: ROOM, WALL, BUILDING

Rare Books Library

Task: Utilizing the previous two exercises as collective research towards a library typology (based upon formal/material/environmental performance) each student was asked to design a rare books library in downtown Boston with an exterior urban space (or landscape) that is open to the public. This particular library is for scholarly research along with a conservation laboratory for early American printed manuscripts and documents. It also has a public auditorium for lectures, a gallery to display the documents, and a cafe.

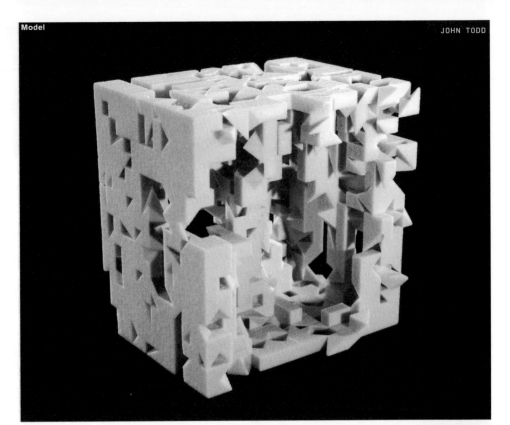

Model

Surface to Mass in Model Elevation

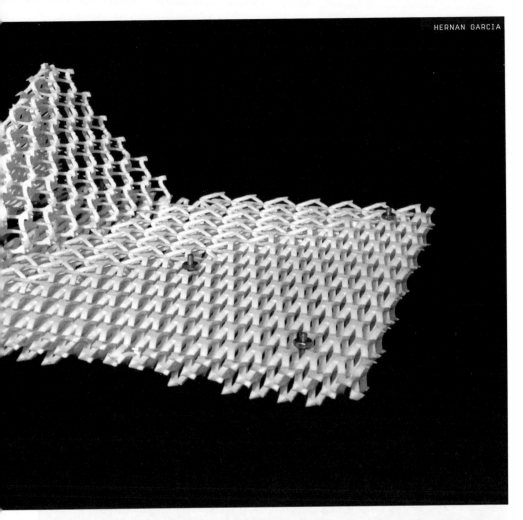

Model   HALLEY WUERTZ

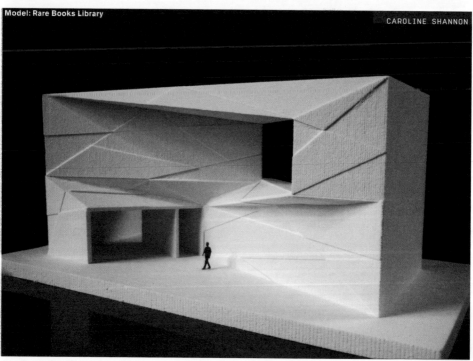

Model: Rare Books Library   CAROLINE SHANNON

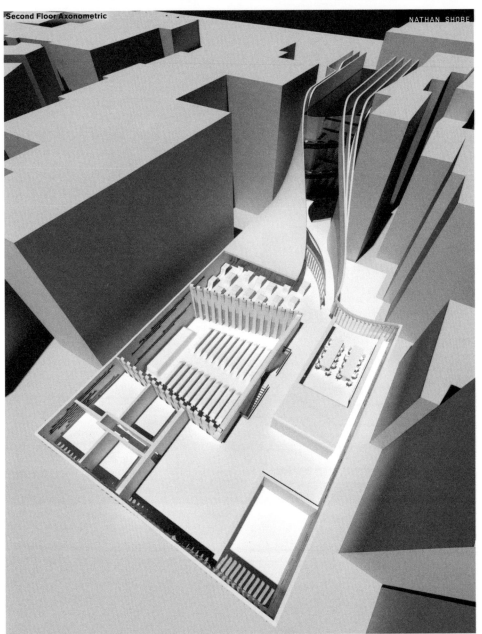

Experiential Section

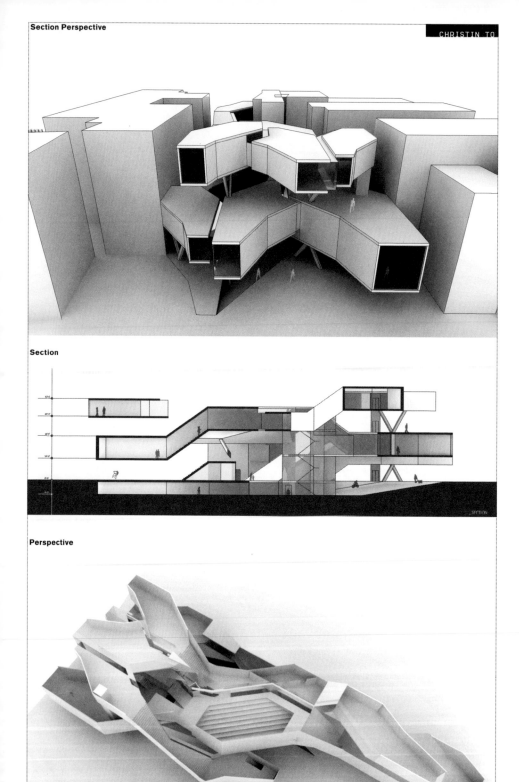

Section

Perspective

Perspective Rendering of Modules

MICHAEL SMITH

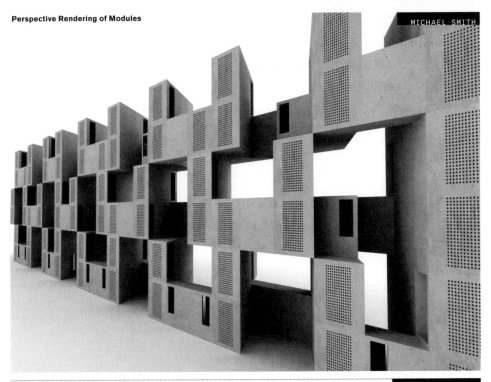

Perspective Drawing

BLAIR CRANSTON

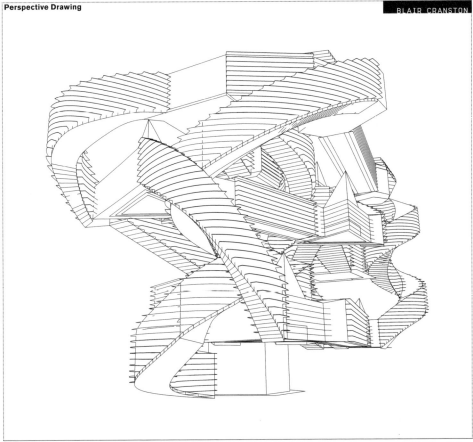

LANDSCAPE ARCHITECTURE II

CORE INSTRUCTORS: ANITA BERRIZBEITIA, HOLLY CLARKE, JILL DESIMINI, MICHAEL VAN VALKENBURGH SPRING 2010

Second semester core studio explores the research and design methods associated with interventions in complex urban conditions: sites layered with multiple interventions across a long span of history that present issues of connectivity, accessibility, identity, and need for contemporary programs. Students learned to apply various forms of research—historical, social, material, spatial, and technical—to the formulation of project arguments and strategies. Emphasis was placed on exploring the relationship between documentation, analytical research, and design through diverse conceptual frameworks and projective representational techniques.

F

W

S

SP

Site Plan + Seasonal Section

Fall, Spring + Summer Sections

EMILY SCHLICKMAN

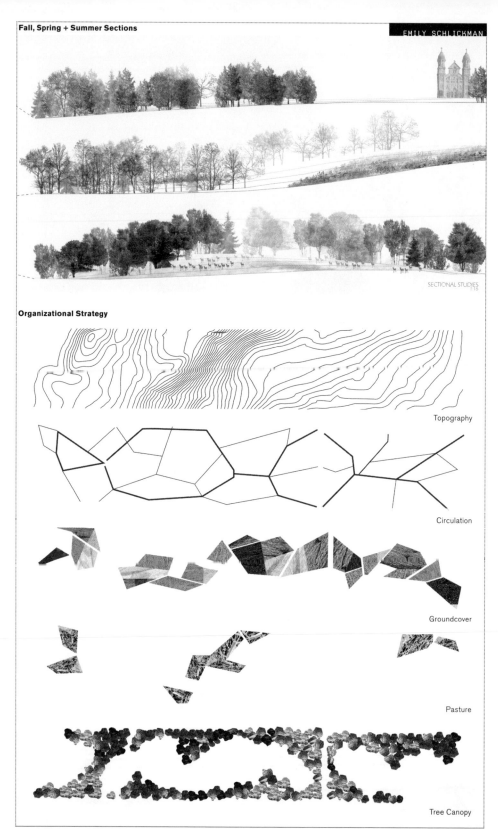

SECTIONAL STUDIES

Organizational Strategy

Topography

Circulation

Groundcover

Pasture

Tree Canopy

Between Park and Agriculture: Experiential Productivity

Between Park and Agriculture: Food Productivity

Kennedy Park Planting Plan

- Trees

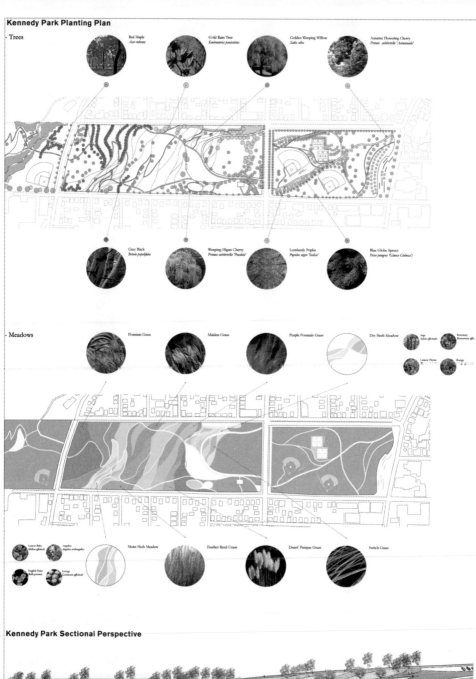

Red Maple
Acer rubrum

Gold Rain Tree
Koelreuteria paniculata

Golden Weeping Willow
Salix alba

Autumn Flowering Cherry
Prunus subhirtella 'Autumnalis'

Grey Birch
Betula populifolia

Weeping Higan Cherry
Prunus subhirtella 'Pendula'

Lombardy Poplar
Populus nigra 'Italica'

Blue Globe Spruce
Picea pungens 'Glauca Globosa'

- Meadows

Fountain Grass

Maiden Grass

Purple Fountain Grass

Dry Herb Meadow

Sage
Salvia officinalis

Rosemary
Rosmarinus officus

Lemon Thyme

Borage

Lemon Balm
Melissa officinalis

Angelica
Angelica archangelica

English Daisy
Bellis perennis

Lovage
Levisticum officinale

Moist Herb Meadow

Feather Reed Grass

Dwarf Pampas Grass

Switch Grass

Kennedy Park Sectional Perspective

Kennedy Park Sections

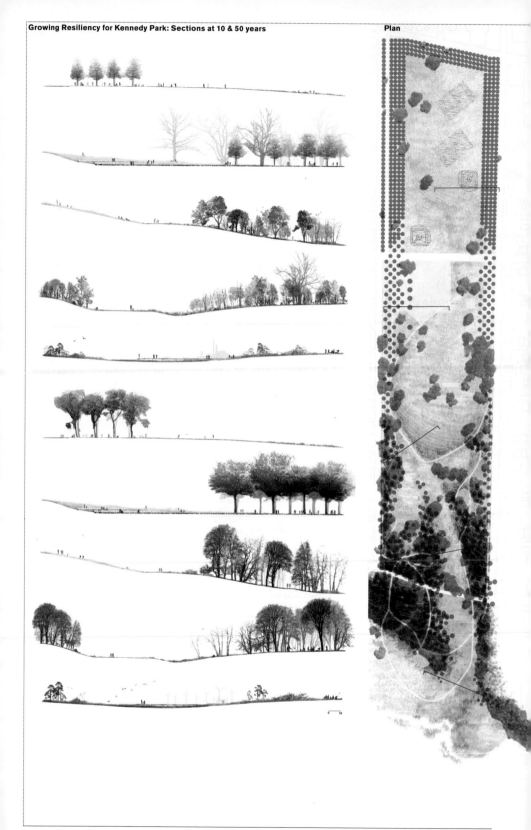

EMILY GORDON

The second semester core planning studio expanded the topics and methodologies studied in the first semester core studio, GSD 1121, aiming to prepare students for the mix of analytical and creative problem-solving needed to address planning issues at the advanced level of the options studios. GSD 1122 centered on a single large-scale planning problem with a regional, intermunicipal scope. The studio addressed the following concerns, all of which are currently central to planning: the pattern and development nature of settlement form; the visual and scenic impact of development either at the fringe or in built-up areas; accessibility, walkability, and the relationship between transit and autos; the location and utility of open space, particularly with respect to development; and the respective roles of large-scale concepts (e.g. plans) vs. regulation in shaping the built environment. The site for the spring studio was Aquidneck Island in the state of Rhode Island, which includes the towns of Portsmouth, Middletown, and Newport. The studio began with two short exercises in Cambridge and Concord and concluded with students creating either a schematic site plan or an infill plan for a fringe or center-city site, respectively.

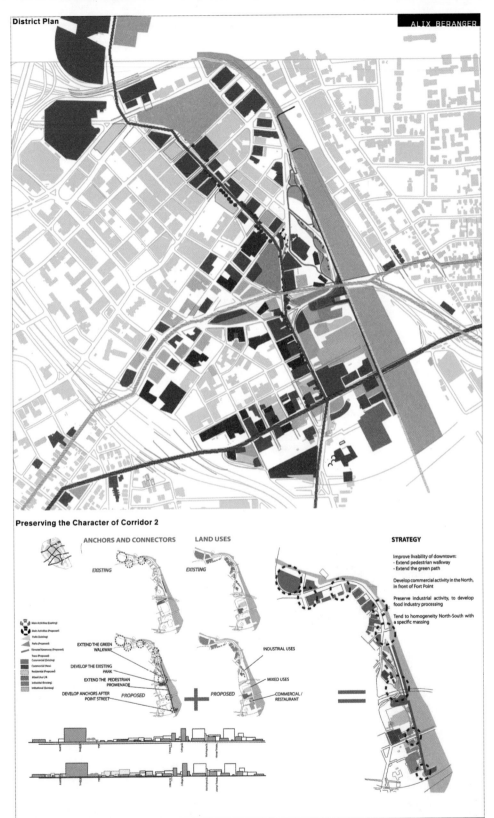

Preserving the Character of Corridor 2

ANCHORS AND CONNECTORS

LAND USES

STRATEGY

Improve livability of downtown:
- Extend pedestrian walkway
- Extend the green path

Develop commercial activity in the North, in front of Fort Point

Preserve industrial activity, to develop food industry processing

Tend to homogeneity North-South with a specific massing

EXISTING

EXISTING

EXTEND THE GREEN WALKWAY

DEVELOP THE EXISTING PARK

EXTEND THE PEDESTRIAN PROMENADE

DEVELOP ANCHORS AFTER POINT STREET

PROPOSED

INDUSTRIAL USES

MIXED USES

COMMERCIAL / RESTAURANT

PROPOSED

Waterfront Park Scene

MICHAEL WILSON

Sectional Progression

SOUTH OF ELM STREET

NORTH OF SOUTH STREET

SOUTH OF SOUTH STREET

NORTH OF POINT STREET

6.5' 24' 6.5'

7' 11' 12' 6'

CARRIE NIELSON

canopy

open space

buildings

infrastructure

fabric

Seamless Providence

CRITICAL ECOLOGIES: ON THE BIOLOGICAL, HORTICULTURAL, AND ANTHROPOLOGICAL ANTECEDENTS TO DESIGN

COLLOQUIUM   CHRIS REED   INTRODUCTORY REMARKS

APRIL 2-3, 2010. EXCERPT

SPEAKERS:
PETER DEL TREDICI, ALEXANDER FELSON, STEVEN HANDEL, KAREN KRAMER, SANFORD KWINTER, SUNE LEHMANN, NINA-MARIE LISTER, PAUL MOORCROFT, MOHSEN MOSTAFAVI, PIET OUDOLF, STEWARD PICKETT, MAXIMILIAN SCHICH, RICHARD WRANGHAM

This event, Critical Ecologies, grew from a number of parallel and occasionally intersecting trajectories.

First, and most obviously, it arose in response to a very general and growing interest in the environment and sustainability the world over, and across the university—caused by an increasing concern about the availability of non-renewable resources, and potential shortages of food and clean water.

Second, it arose in response to a broad resurgence of interest in ecology and ecological thinking in design research, pedagogy, and practice, including a number of very recent and vigorous discussions at the GSD and in and among its multiple departments. Here I note the importance of last spring's Ecological Urbanism conference in igniting and re-framing broader interdisciplinary conversations around these issues.

Third, it arose in response to a series of discussions that have been unfolding in a number of research seminars, design studios, meetings, and conferences around issues of adaptation, open-endedness, succession, and—perhaps most provocatively—the curatorial potential of ecological practices. These discussions are of particular interest to those of us in landscape, a discipline perhaps uniquely situated to leverage ecology—writ broadly—as both medium and as conceptual model, as instrument and as idea.

Finally, it grew from a lineage of design and planning practices that, in different ways, have taken on the project of the environment and ecology as central, as an essential driver, in the framing of urban projects, of adaptive architectural elements, of ephemeral experiments.

Given all this, the colloquium is an attempt to probe more deeply into the current status of ecology and its allied fields (biology, horticulture, anthropology), in an effort to get beneath the surface of ecological sciences to explore untapped potentials for design. It is also an effort to reflect critically about advances in related disciplines that have taken on ideas about resiliency, dynamism, and open-endedness in ways that might further enrich design thinking and design practices.

So why critical? And why ecologies (plural)?

Very simply, this framing is a recognition of what I understand to be a plurality of ecological theory and research: landscape ecology, human ecology, urban ecology, applied ecology, restoration ecology, deep ecology, the neutral theory of ecology are but a few of the specialized areas of research that have emerged over the past decades and continue to inform about thinking about the various interrelationships between plants, animals, and the physical, biological world we live in.

Yet it's also a recognition of a very tight alignment—again, as I see it—between these ideas and current thinking about human adaptation and evolution (which we'll see demonstrated in the work of Richard Wrangham); about characteristics of emergence (as documented in the writings of folks like Steven Johnson); about the behavior of dynamic networks (as in the work of Albert-Laszlo Barabasi and others); and about complex adaptive systems—no matter their discipline.

ANITA BERRIZBEITIA, NINA-MARIE LISTER, STEWARD PICKETT

RICHARD WRANGHAM SANFORD KWINTER

Colloquium Describe Identity

SOME ASSEMBLAGE REQUIRED: A CONVENTION CENTER IN EAST DETROIT

M ARCH THESIS ERIN KASIMOW

ADVISOR: MACK SCOGIN

This thesis seeks to define the moment a building's original purpose comes to an end not as one of obsolescence but as the potential for a new point of origin in the building's existence. It explores the idea of regenerative architecture based on opportunities within the unscripted afterlife of a building.

—Mack Scogin

This project entailed the designed demolition of the Packard Plant in Detroit. Conceived as a 100-year process, a convention center is located on the site to host events and projected inhabitations and architectural constructs as the building is breaking down due to man-made and naturally occurring entropic processes.

At the Packard Plant, regeneration and rereading of spaces is enabled by the very processes, mechanisms, and spatial circumstance that are contributing to the building's natural decay, fragmentation, and breaking down. The visual sequence, sensorial experiences, and unbelievable circumstances of the Packard Plant causes a deep questioning of context, scale, and spatial definition. No longer defined by the programmatic constraints of assembly and production, spatial zones are demarcated by ephemeral and often inverted parameters—light, texture, surface—that are in constant transition. One's senses are heightened as elements taken for granted; color, sound, and texture are unbelievably exaggerated and ambiguous.

The proposed constructs and scenarios seek to project potential inhabitations and transformations using the spatial logics and processes currently at play on the site. They do not attempt to coalesce into an overall big picture or master planning scheme but rather represent a collection of opportunities or regenerative moments drawn from the conditions of the site and from which new spatial readings and futures of the site could occur. Some are about instigating a result or effect based on exacerbating entropic processes, while others are about defining or celebrating a space before it's gone. The intention of the thesis is to operate within a logic of constant change and indeterminacy. While there may be deliberate construction of spaces, the definition of these spaces is subject to processes of decay and the collective agreement of visitors and inhabitants of the building, preserving the lack of authority that defines the Packard's afterlife.

Model

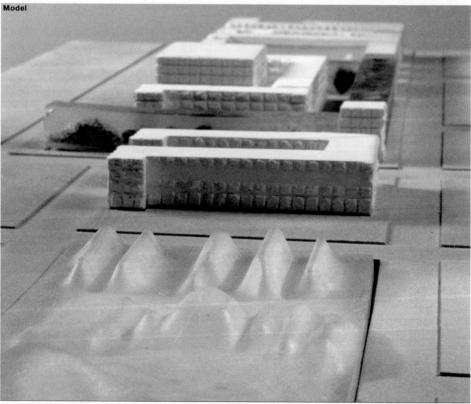

Model

Exhibition Hall: Growth

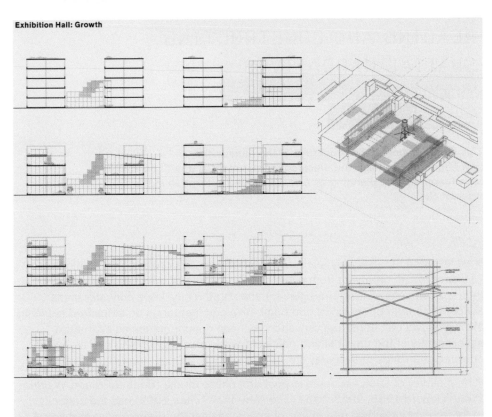

Ballroom

READING AND CONSTRUCTING
SPATIAL NARRATIVES

MUP THESIS | CHRISTINA CALABRESE

ADVISOR: BRENT RYAN

This thesis examines the positions of the flaneur, the psychogeographer, and the placelogger as potential positions for a reappraisal of planning as a spacemaking enterprise in the modern city.

—Brent Ryan

If we leverage the everyday accounts of urban life—the profane intersections of perspectives on urbanism from residents and visitors of urban environments— then we can compel new strategies for shaping the city. If we consider these accounts as both cooperative and combative commentaries on actualized planning strategies, we can constructively channel these commentaries as alternative assessments of the physical and political frameworks challenging and supporting social relationships in everyday life.

A brief survey of such accounts in print and online media (Baudelaire and Waldrop 2009; Debord 1955, 1957, 1958; *The New York Times* 2009) has the capacity to foreground individual use values of space against the predominant exchange values of space driving global city design configurations today. What can emerge is a matrix of socio-spatial transgressions and fortifications of connectivity that subverts the imposition of static, divisive land use plans. This connectivity accommodates the individual experience and agency of urban dwellers as a structuring device for the city to develop dynamically, daily.

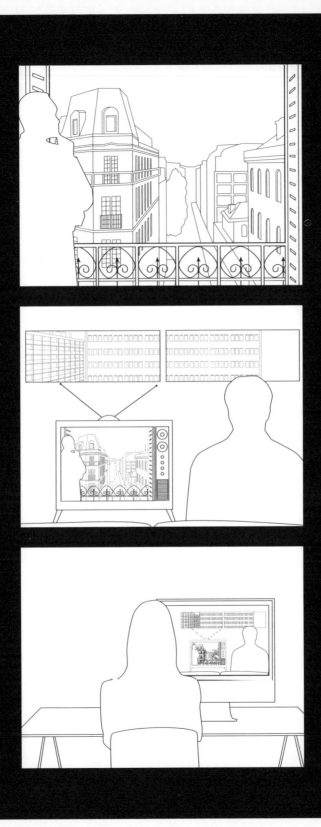

WHERE'S ALICE?

"Fairy tales can come true, it can happen to you...if you're young at heart."
—Carolyn Leigh

The iPhone and Swiss Army knife are commercial product equivalents to the fantastical fairy tale and ballad. They are figments of the imagination designed to at once suspend and initiate reinterpretation, rearrangement, and redevelopment. Of these forms, the iPhone (and its aspirants) is arguably the most innately transformative. It changes human behavior. Its generative potentials include, among others: experiential complexity, micro and macro economies, community definition, technological innovation and networks and vocabularies of communication. In addition, it can be morphed into a variety of alternative implements from a musical instrument to a camera to a way-finding device to a gaming center—an immense tool for social order into which the individual finds place (space) and identity (distinction).

The traditional role of architecture has been to reposition the individual against society.

This studio investigated the possibilities of an architecture that inherently possesses the spatial, functional, and spiritual richness of a social order empowered by the individual.

It included film and music retrospectives, visiting inquisitors, thesis statements, architectural app concepts, angst, field trip(s), site selections by each student, individualized program assignments, bewilderment, fun, research and rigor.

Option Studio Describe Identity

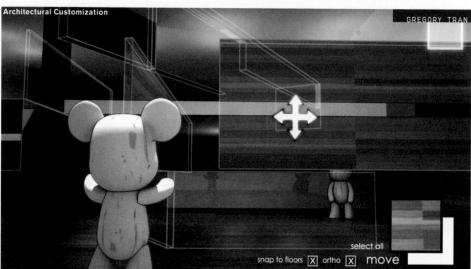

Architectural Customization

snap to floors [X] ortho [X] move

select all

Leonardo at the Museum (Augmented Reality and Architecture)

Simultaneity of Space

M12 69490

7023
3556 swpbonus
lvl+3677

Describe Identity **Option Studio**

154

View of Casino from Roof

MARIKA SHIOIRI-CLARK

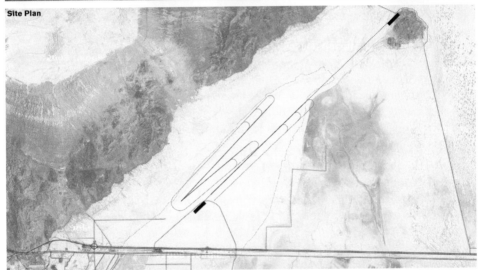

Site Plan

View Out to Deck

Option Studio Describe Identity

INSERT!
CHINATOWN LIBRARY

STUDENT RESEARCH

PROJECT TEAM

MARRIKKA TROTTER, QUILIAN RIANO, JULIAN BUSHMAN-COPP, TREVOR PATT, MATTHEW SWAIDAN, SHELBY DOYLE, DAN HUI, MO LEE, JUNGMIN NAM, THERESA HWANG, STEPHANIE TAM, ANDREW THOMAS, JAMES DELANEY, MARIA SANTOS, JONATHAN SANTOS, ALICIA TAYLOR, KATHLEEN THORNTON, JEGAN VINCENT DE PAUL, JONATHAN EVANS, STEWART GOHRING, ANNIE KOUNTZ, LAURA SNOWDON, LELAND COTT

DONORS

SHAWMUT DESIGN AND CONSTRUCTION, IN PARTNERSHIP WITH BENT ELECTRICAL CONTRACTORS, ANGELINI PLASTERING, AND MARK RICHEY WOODWORKING, MAHARAM, COMPASS FLOORING, TONY KWAN, GSD STUDENT FORUM AND SOCIAL CHANGE AND ACTIVISM

INSERT is a student group founded in the spring of 2009 for GSD students seeking a place to design, fund, and fabricate small public projects in local communities. The first project by INSERT was the design and construction of a temporary program system for the Chinatown Storefront Library, which transformed an empty storefront in Boston's Chinatown into a temporary public library. Operating for four months, the project provided urgently needed services for a community that has been without a library since 1956, while creating a new advocacy tool for Chinatown's efforts for a permanent library.

The INSERT team consisted of twelve GSD students who collaboratively designed, fundraised for, and fabricated a temporary spatial installation that accommodated children's reading and storytelling, internet access, and multi-lingual book and periodical areas targeting Chinatown's large elderly population. The design is modular, portable, and reconfigurable; adapting to multiple locations and changes in use. Since the Storefront Library closed at the end of January 2010, the installation has been reconfigured and reused in a high school library and an early childcare center, both in the Chinatown community.

Student Research Describe Identity

THE VERTICAL GARDEN, FROM NATURE TO THE CITY

MARGARET MCCURRY LECTURE IN THE DESIGN ARTS

PATRICK BLANC NOVEMBER 3, 2009. EXCERPT

To make a vertical garden is very easy, because you basically just have to staple a kind of felt onto a plastic sheet. Everybody can do it. The technique is very simple. What's important to know is *what* to staple on to that plastic sheet because a garden is made of plants.

I always use the plants that grow in nature on slopes, on cliffs, and on rocks. And, unless I am working in a tropical country, tropical plants are only for indoor projects. Indoors, around the world is about 20 degrees: You can be in Bangkok, or in Alaska, it is always about the same. It is very uniform between indoor projects.

But outdoors there is a lot of variety because the species depend on the specific location. Everywhere that it's possible, I like to use native plants and those species are dependent on what the plants can withstand. For instance, if I am doing a garden in Spain, I don't use the same species as I do in the South of France, the North of France, Japan, New York, or San Francisco, because, of course, the climate is different.

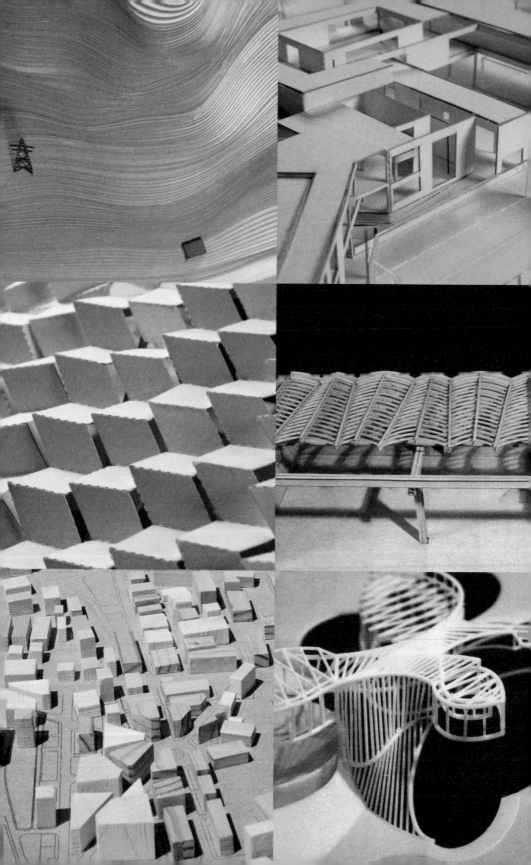

Construct Equality

The work in this section explores the power of design to address some of the world's disparities through awareness, resistance, and physical change. Here, the projects illustrate how engaging the political through design can achieve better lives through better environments, provide opportunities for justice by making it spatial, and offer far-reaching results by rethinking even the smallest detail.

CAN WE LEAVE THE BAUXITE IN THE MOUNTAIN?

LECTURE ARUNDHATI ROY APRIL 1, 2010. EXCERPT

I used to say that dissent is India's best export and that we have to globalize dissent. Many of the corporations we are fighting are headquartered in places like America or Germany, so we need activists working there.

While that still needs to happen, I realized that actually the only battles that are being won are battles where people fight locally. But here there's a problem too. You can barricade yourself locally and militantly if the government wants to take your land from you, but what if they are building a dam far away and the only thing that is going to take your land is that river that rises? You can't fire bullets at it. An arms struggle doesn't work unless you can stop the first foundation stone being laid.

So I think, every issue, every ecosystem, every kind of geography has a different kind of resistance that is effective. You can't be a Ghandian in the forest because no one is watching and you can't really be a Maoist in the road because you'll just be killed. We need a whole biodiversity of resistance.

BUILDING
THE TEMPORARY CONCERT HALL
IN L'AQUILA

OPTION STUDIO | SHIGERU BAN, DANIELLE ETZLER

In general, architects work for the privileged. Historically, we have served religious and noblemen, and now corporations and governments employ us to display their power. In this, our engagement with the general public is limited by our association with monuments and the rich. When natural disasters occur, architects have a responsibility to contribute to the repair of buildings that have failed, and to create shelter to house those in need. The objective of the studio was to engage students in the responsive act of designing and of building that which is necessary.

In April 2009, the city of L'Aquila, Italy, was devastated by an earthquake that displaced more than 60,000 residents and completely destroyed the center of the medieval city. Although the Italian government quickly provided various forms of temporary housing outside the city, more than a year later the historic center of L'Aquila remains quarantined and in rubble, without a comprehensive rebuilding plan. The vibrant street life of city is absent in exchange for fences and scaffolding that will remain for years to come as the rebuilding efforts take shape.

The events of February 2010 brought the attention of the studio to Haiti as a point of departure for making work that is both socially relevant and urgent. A 4-meter by 4-meter tent was designed and fabricated, then sent as a prototype to be used for a community of 50 families in Port Au Prince.

The prototype project for Haiti was followed by a trip to L'Aquila, where the studio met with local residents and officials to understand the extent of the devastation and what would be most useful to the city. Students developed their own projects in pairs, in most cases building at full scale to realize work that could immediately impact a community in need.

Interior View of the Shelter

HSIANGHENG CHUNG, XIAOYING MA

Prototype

JON SARGENT, LAURA VIKLUND

Construct Equality **Option Studio**

AIMEE EPSTEIN, MARCELA DELGADO

Option Studio Construct Equality

PROJECT LINK

STUDENT RESEARCH

FOUNDERS
ANDY LANTZ, JON EVANS

INSTRUCTORS
ANDREW BRYAN, JON EVANS, ANDY LANTZ, SARA QUEEN, JASON PHIPPS,
NAOMI TOUGER, JULIAN BUSHMAN-COPP, KELLY MANGOLD, ANNIE KOUNTZ,
MIRIAM EL RASSI, DEREK CHAN, JUSTIN BROWN, HYE-VIN KIM, NORA YOO,
ELIZABETH BACON, HALLIE CHEN, EVANGELOS KOTSIORIS,
AMY WHITESIDES, MARIKA SHIOIRI-CLARK

PROJECT LINK is an outreach, research, and educational initiative that allows the GSD Community to proactively engage its local surroundings. Founded by the student group Social Change and Activism (SoCA), the program immerses Boston area youth in the world of design by exposing them to drawing, modeling, and representation techniques associated with architecture, landscape architecture, graphic design, industrial design, and fine arts. Through studio based investigations, PROJECT LINK strives to foster design skills and conceptual thinking in order to put students on track for exploring these ideas at the collegiate level. By exposing students to the possibilities offered through a design education, the program provides them with the agency to imagine how design can transform their lives and their environments.

PROJECT LINK has been created, planned, and initiated by graduate students in the fields of Architecture, Landscape Architecture, and Urban Planning at the Graduate School of Design, with input and collaboration from students at Harvard's Graduate School of Education. It is a student-run and university-funded opportunity that extends an inspiring hand into Boston communities to help provide opportunities to underprivileged and talented middle and high school students. There are three different studio based programs that fall under the umbrella of PROJECT LINK: Design Initiative for Youth (DiY), a semester-long studio for middle school students, PROJECT LINK Summer Studio, a four-week intensive studio for high school students, and LINK LiTE, a semester-long college preparatory studio for Project Link Alumni. This network of programs seeks to take action in challenging the stark diversity statistic found in the profession and throughout most architectural educational programs by providing multiple pre-collegiate opportunities to participate within the field of design to those who would otherwise not be exposed to it.

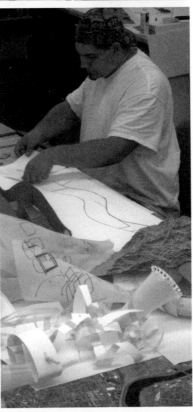

REDEVELOPMENT POLICY

SEMINAR   SUSAN FAINSTEIN

Urban redevelopment is the process by which government, private investors, and households transform the uses and financial returns of the urban built environment. As an area of public policy, it is a response to the perceived deterioration of cities caused by initial poor construction, decay, economic restructuring, regional shifts, suburbanization, and social segregation. Different social groups receive different costs and benefits as a consequence of redevelopment efforts. The objective of this course was to examine the process of urban decline, the kinds of responses it has evoked, the principal redevelopment actors, the possible range of redevelopment strategies, and the social and spatial impacts of redevelopment efforts.

Jackson Heights, Queens, NY: revitalization by immigration

London: Stratford, site of the 2012 Olympics

Amsterdam Bijlmermeer: original construction and new infill

Lowell, MA: redevelopment of downtown

Paris: old wine warehouse, recycled as retail district

Shanghai: historic district recreated as shopping mall

CONCERNING THE USER:
THE EXPERIMENT OF MODERN URBANISM
IN POSTWAR FRANCE 1955-1975

PHD THESIS | KENNY CUPERS

ADVISORS: ANTOINE PICON, MARGARET CRAWFORD

Kenny presents a radically new interpretation of the French "Grands Ensembles," those postwar mass-housing programs that have often been seen as purely technocratic endeavors. In a path-breaking analysis, he reveals how important was the consideration of the user as well as concerns for a regenerated social life.

—Antoine Picon

If there is one master narrative about the postwar European city, it is most likely that of the high hopes and ultimate failures of modern urbanism. This evolution has come to be understood as a logical consequence of its authoritarian denial of user needs. Caught up in rhetoric and critique, the history of this "banal modernism" has meanwhile remained remarkably overlooked. Focusing on French mass housing estates and new towns, this dissertation examines the development of modern urbanism and its mounting criticisms through the lens of what turns out to be a shared concern: the user.

Under the influence of an expanding welfare state and a rising consumer culture during France's postwar decades of unprecedented economic and urban growth, the user became an increasingly central question in the organization of everyday life. The study reveals how modern urbanism was shaped by and actively shaped this development, in which the user shifted from a standard, passive beneficiary of public services to an active participant and demanding consumer.

The dissertation argues that French urbanism evolved as an experimental process in which the realms of production and consumption were in continual interaction. Amongst the cultures of urban expertise, the domain of sociology became a central mediator in this process. Providing architects and planners with a unique entryway into the world of the user, it informed the design of new housing typologies and urban centers meant to entice users in novel ways.

Prevailing accounts tend to cast the postwar French city either as shaped by a degenerated version of interwar modernism or driven by the exigencies of a centralized state. This study develops an alternative focus: rather than architectural doctrine or government policy, it is the changing category of the user—fueled by the entanglement of social welfare and consumer culture—that underlies the politics of urban change in postwar France. By showing how expertise of the user traverses what have previously been understood as fundamentally opposing approaches to the city—modernist technocratic planning versus user participation—the study dismantles the notions of "top-down" and "bottom-up" that continue to shape urban debates today.

Evry I "Les Pyramids", by Michel Andrault and Pierre Parat, 1971–1974

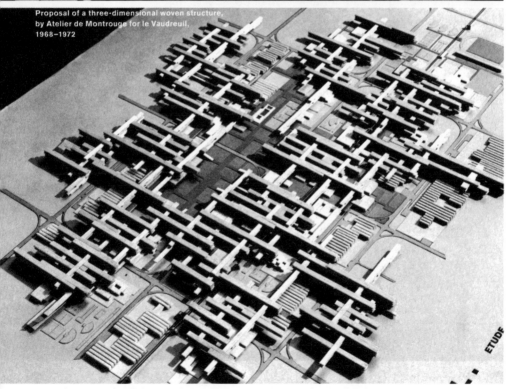

Proposal of a three-dimensional woven structure, by Atelier de Montrouge for le Vaudreuil, 1968–1972

Image Sources: Claude Parent, "Interview, Andrault & Parat" *L'Architecture*, no. 403 (1977): 92-104; "Le Vaudreuil: Une méthode d'étude et de réalisation" *Cahiers de l'IAURP* 30(1973): 51 & 54

CAMBRIDGE TALKS

SYMPOSIUM   ANTOINE PICON   INTRODUCTORY REMARKS   APRIL 16-17, 2010

SPEAKERS:
DANIEL B. MONK, MOHSEN MOSTAFAVI, SHEILA JASANOFF,
LAWRENCE VALE, NASSER RABBAT, KATE HOLLIDAY,
AMY SLATON, PANAYIOTA PYLA, VIRAG MOLNAR, RAFI SEGAL,
AJANTHA SUBRAMANIAN

One thing to note immediately is that the relations between design and politics have varied a lot, to say the least, in the recent past. To make a long and complex history short, I would say that this somewhat tortuous path is linked to the desire to avoid two symmetric pitfalls. The first is the naïve belief that politics as we know it can find a direct translation in design. The second, the attempt to transform design into a perfectly neutral expertise, as if such expertise could exist. To put it another way, this second risk is about believing that design may be or have the solution. Design is never the solution; it may contribute to solve issues, but never alone.

The complexity of the history of the relation between design and politics in the recent past has to do with these recurring risks. On the one hand, one has the risk to interpret design as a mere tool enabling the direct translation of political issues in spatial terms; on the other, one faces the danger that goes with the belief that one may have the solution.

Now, the post-September 11 world is definitely more aware that violence and suffering exist and must be addressed in other terms than the generalizations we have used in the past. The post-Katrina storm and post-Haiti earthquake world is more aware than ever of the existence of catastrophes and the need for design to deal with them. We now know that the environment represents a daunting challenge that will more and more often translate in political and social terms.

In this world, design is leaning towards a more serious engagement with the political. But the question is how to do that without falling into the two previous traps.

Between the risk of becoming a tool and the danger of appearing as a solution, a whole set of new attitudes has been made possible. They all revolve around the central issue of agency.

Design possesses an agency that is irreducible to other forms of approaches. It should be neither hegemonic nor passively obedient. Its agency lies rather in its capacity to displace frontiers, to reformulate problems.

This symposium should be not only about what is political in design, but also about how designers can be players in the political arena and about how politics should enter into a conversation with them. This is not a simple question.

If one takes an exterior look at designers, one is often tempted to see them in a double and contradictory light that has something to do with the polarity between design as instrument and design as solution that I evoked at the beginning of my presentation.

On the one hand, there is a tendency to look down sometimes at designers, as if they were specialists of a somewhat esoteric domain. On the other hand, who are those people who have the audacity to think that they have solutions, who feel entitled to design the spaces in which we have to live?

Now, this mix of power and lack of power takes its full sense in the light of what might be ultimately what design is about as a political activity: restraint. Here I would like to propose restraint as what enables us to avoid those pitfalls. Restraint from totally submitting design to ordinary politics, but also restraint from the temptation of pure autonomy.

Design is political when it learns how to assert its power but also how to recognize and play upon its limitations. Design is political when it knows how to restrain itself.

TB CLINICS
AND RESEARCH LABORATORIES
IN ETHIOPIA

OPTION STUDIO | PETER ROSE

The studio project consisted of two parts: a central TB Clinic and Research Laboratory in Addis Ababa (capital city of Ethiopia) and a connected network of smaller Rural TB Treatment Centers dispersed throughout this large country of 85 million people.

PART A

MAIN PROGRAM. A 200 bed TB Clinic and Research Laboratory to be located on or near the grounds of Addis Ababa University. This clinic will be the headquarters and coordination center for a network of smaller clinics to be located in as many as 30 rural communities throughout the country.

ADDITIONAL PROGRAM. Space for patients co-infected with HIV AIDS; spaces for a small library, conference, teleconference, art and other educational programs; and a landscape, which will be integral programmatically, architecturally, and medically to the project.

SPECIAL REQUIREMENTS. Critically important for TB treatment, and typically lacking in facilities in Ethiopia, are a high volume of fresh air, substantial amounts of controlled daylight, and moderate temperatures (achieved in western countries with complex mechanical systems). The studio devised sustainable strategies for these requirements, using the architecture itself and minimal mechanical systems.

PART B

A prototype 10 to 20 bed TB Clinic and Research Laboratory designed to be prefabricated, transportable, modifiable to local needs and conditions, to be set up in as many as 30 rural communities throughout the country.

Architecture cannot, by itself, cure TB. However, intelligently and systemically conceived, as part of a connected network of medical, technical, political, cultural, and human resources, it can be extraordinarily effective.

The challenge of the studio was to invent an architecture of lean, sustainable, strategic buildings—easily built and modifiable using local materials and methods, mostly cast concrete and timber, or buildings that can be prefabricated, transported to a site, and locally assembled. Though these buildings would be instruments of desperately needed change, the studio strived to go beyond the needs of pure "science" and "function" to make structures and spaces that were beautiful and uplifting as well.

Perspective: Public Access

Perspective: Plaza

"You should spatialize whatever you are doing, and this will lead to interesting insights in a very assertive and vigorous way. Spatial thinking can not only enrich our understanding of almost any subject, but it also has the added potential to extend our practical knowledge into more effective actions, and to make theoretical breakthroughs that one could never imagine otherwise.

Not just an incidental spatial perspective, or a look at space just as pure physical form, or as a dimension of things, but space as a forceful actor, and part of the protest in struggling against injustices."

"There are rights that are associated with living in cities whether one is a stranger, a migrant, a citizen or not, that allows one to have an appeal to have a fair share of the resources that cities generate. And given that the economic geographers and geographical economists are telling us that urban agglomerations are the primary cause of all economic development, technological innovation, and cultural creativity, the cities generate a lot and there is a lot at stake for these rights to the city."

GLOBAL REDESIGN PROJECT I: LE KINKELIBA

OPTION STUDIO | TOSHIKO MORI

SPONSORS: ELISE JAFFE AND JEFF BROWN

Le Kinkeliba is a small but highly successful bottom-up medical and educational NGO aid organization founded in 1995 by Dr. Gilles Degois of Paris. Le Kinkeliba's projects are located in a remote and fragile rural region of south eastern Senegal, West Africa. The region lies south of Tambacounda, along the Gambia River and adjacent to Niokolo Koba National Park to the east, a UNESCO Biosphere Reserve. The local community suffers from high rates of maternal mortality, malaria, infant mortality, and other treatable diseases.

From the outset, Dr. Degois recognized the need to acknowledge the connectivity of the region's problems and the holistic solutions that would be required to address them. Therefore the eight facilities established to date include medical clinics, a maternal health clinic, a kindergarten, a girls' residence and a farm school.

Today, Le Kinkeliba operates this network with an entirely Senegalese staff of highly trained, dedicated doctors, nurses, midwives, teachers, and specialists. This successful micro-organizational system empowers its community at the same time that it offers economic sustainability, education, and health care. It is a small yet powerful example of a rural organization that confronts and solves a community's complex and multifaceted issues in an efficient, caring, and ecological manner.

Le Kinkeliba's next project—the subject of the studio—is the Kinkeliba Foundation. In 2005, Le Kinkeliba was given a site of nearly 100 acres by the Senegalese government, lying just 10 miles south of Le Kinkeliba's original medical center. The site, overlooking the Gambia River, was the setting of this new initiative. It offered visual and performance artists, writers, scholars, and others from all over the world a unique opportunity to converge in an extraordinary setting and work independently and inter-dependently. The project was specific to the community of Le Kinkeliba but it touched upon the universal issues relating to the development of smaller, thus more humanely scaled rural communities.

The studio worked on a plan for self-sustaining infrastructure, at a micro and macro scale. Building prototypes were developed to consider the choice of materials and methods of fabrication, in consideration of the location's resources, skill, and labor availability. An assembling sequence and permutation of components were studied with an emphasis of "loose fit" and "informal assembly" to allow for ad-hoc and improvisational results. The studio sought innovation through the imaginative use of local materials and techniques. Le Kinkeliba's operational, social, and organizational ingenuity was studied to reflect future scalable potential.

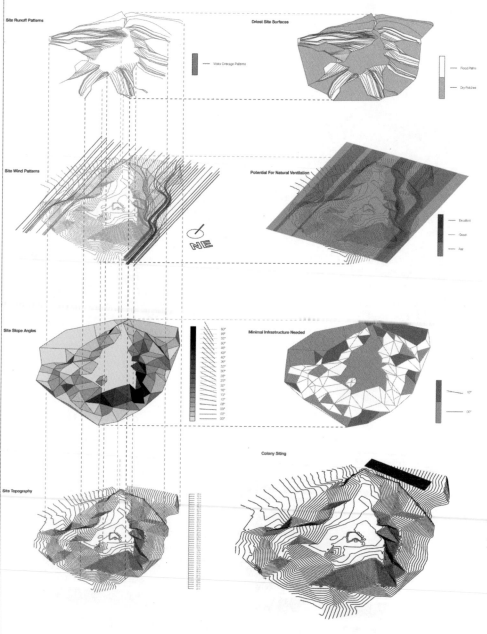

Site Runoff Patterns

Water Drainage Patterns

Driest Site Surfaces

Flood Paths

Dry Patches

Site Wind Patterns

NE

Potential For Natural Ventilation

Excellent

Good

Fair

Site Slope Angles

Minimal Infrastructure Needed

10°

00°

Colony Siting

Site Topography

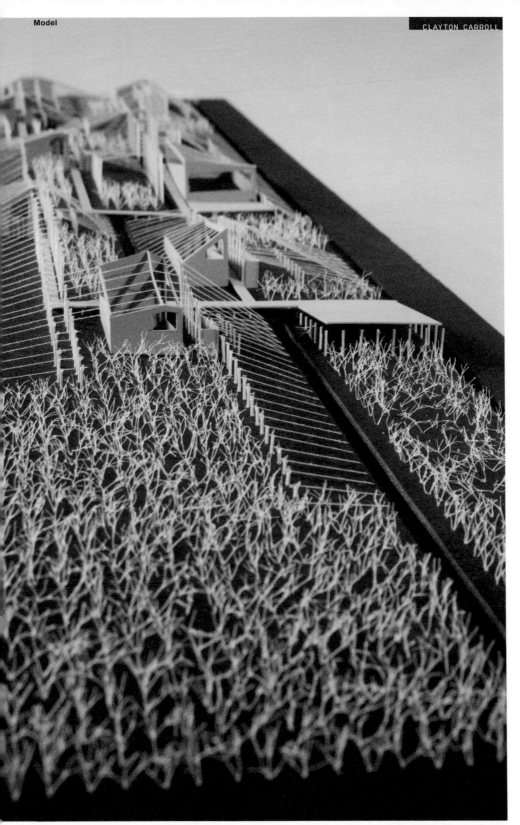

Option Studio Construct Equality

Construct Equality **Option Studio**

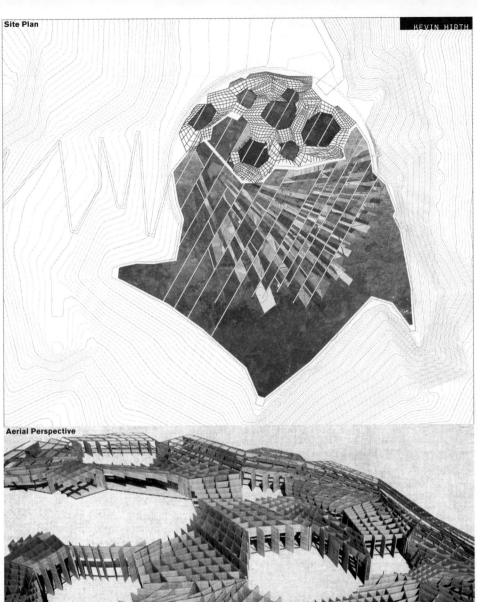

Aerial Perspective

MAX BOND, MULTICULTURALISM AND SOCIAL EQUALITY IN THE BUILT ENVIRONMENT

SYMPOSIUM OCTOBER 2, 2009, EXCERPT

SPEAKERS:
CRAIG BARTON, PETER COOK, JONATHAN EVANS,
ANTHONY SCHUMAN

Max served as a forerunner for a new approach to architecture and through the strength of his convictions, in his leadership, in his teaching, in his service, and in his practice, Max helped to shape us into a profession that is more inclusive, more democratic, and better than the way he found it.

—Anthony Schuman

He really believed in the role of architecture, the role of public spaces and public places as catalysts for the transformation of our societal needs. This is work that which he did, not only through buildings, not only through architecture, but also through his professional advocacy, his public service, and his teaching.

—Mohsen Mostafavi

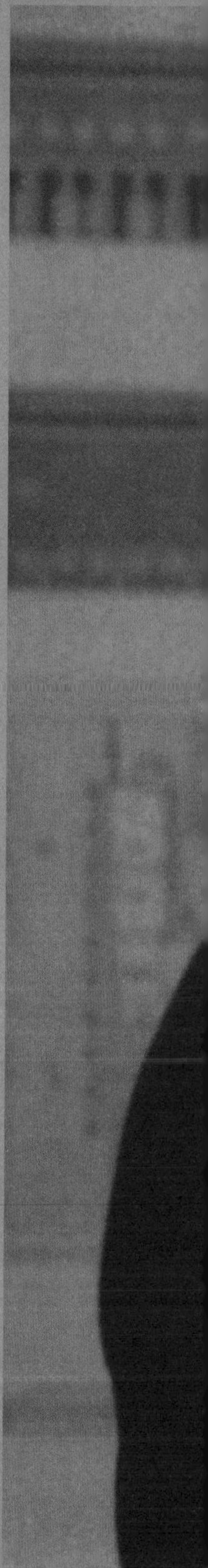

It was the first time I became aware of the heights and accomplishments of architects who looked like me, but most importantly I was awakened to the fact that my new found profession came with a sense of purpose.

—Toni Griffin

Max was an ally, both within society at large and within our profession. Max stood for architecture's social vocation. He speaks as an architect, he works as an architect, and that was the focal point of his working day, but he was after larger objectives, going to the root of social, economic, and cultural issues that set the larger framework for design's more modest role.

—Craig Barton

CITIES OF GOLD: ADAPTIVE INFRASTRUCTURE FOR POST-GOLD JOHANNESBURG AND EKURHULENI, SOUTH AFRICA

MLA THESIS | DOROTHY TANG

ADVISOR: CHRISTIAN WERTHMANN

Dorothy's thesis dwells on the sardonic adjacency of a massive gold extraction belt next to some of the most resource deprived slums in Johannesburg. By not letting the gold companies off the hook, she sets a new deal in motion—strategically switch land, and let toxicity be the guideline for a new remediation landscape that also mitigates many of the slum dwellers' miseries.

—Christian Werthmann

Since the Witwatersrand Gold rush of 1886, the urban form of Johannesburg and Ekurhuleni has been intimately tied to global gold prices, mining, and waste. Deep shaft gold mining has actively altered the topography, hydrology, and ecosystems of the 80-km mining belt that traverses the region. In the 1970's, the decline of the mining industry set the stage for informal settlements to invade former mining lands. The degraded environmental conditions are major obstacles for these communities to improve their livelihood. Recent advances in technology and escalating gold prices have enabled additional gold recovery from mine dumps scattered throughout the city, activating substantial topographical and hydrological changes. These operations release land back into the market. This project suggests that the rehabilitation process of this post-gold landscape will set the stage for productive urban growth that privileges vulnerable communities. Scarce water resources are a critical entry point for landscape interventions, especially with the treatment of wastewater and acid mine drainage, and should continue to perform despite the fluctuation of industries, politics, and the economy.

The project catalogues unique landscape conditions in the undermined areas of the mining belt and responds accordingly based on occupancy, soil contamination, infrastructural needs, and the threat of acid mine drainage. The proposal puts forth a set of scenarios that respond to each condition, their consequences, and opportunities for convergence over time.

As a collection, these four strategies will produce a landscape that will continue to support the urban growth of Johannesburg in a productive way. The process of remediating a post-gold landscape becomes the platform for economical, social, and ecological viability of the region.

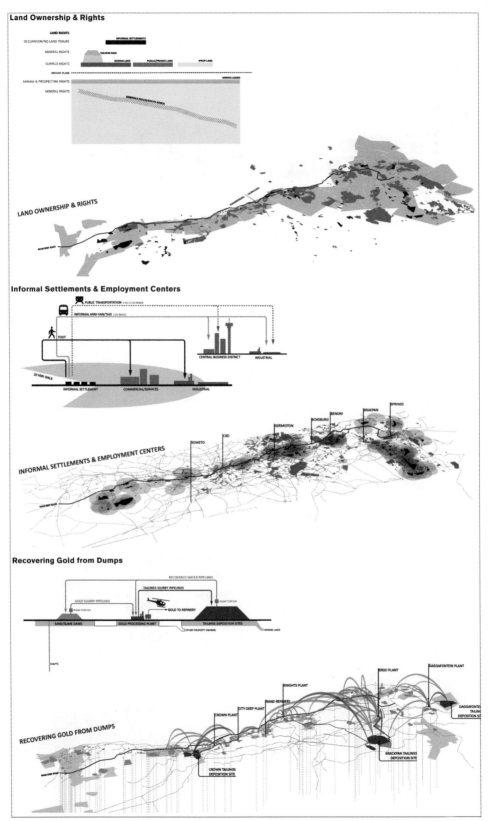

Land Ownership & Rights

LAND RIGHTS

OCCUPATION/NO LAND TENURE	INFORMAL SETTLEMENTS	
MINERAL RIGHTS	TAILINGS DAM	
SURFACE RIGHTS	MINING LAND	PUBLIC/PRIVATE LAND	IPROP LAND
GROUND PLANE		
MINING & PROSPECTING RIGHTS		MINING LEASES
MINERAL RIGHTS		MINERALS TOPCO/SOUTH AFRICA

LAND OWNERSHIP & RIGHTS

MAIN REEF ROAD

Informal Settlements & Employment Centers

PUBLIC TRANSPORTATION 9.95-17.00 RANDS
INFORMAL MINI-VAN/TAXI 5.00 RANDS
FOOT

20 MIN WALK

CENTRAL BUSINESS DISTRICT   INDUSTRIAL

INFORMAL SETTLEMENT   COMMERCIAL/SERVICES   INDUSTRIAL

INFORMAL SETTLEMENTS & EMPLOYMENT CENTERS

SOWETO   CBD   GERMISTON   BOKSBURG   BENONI   BRAKPAN   SPRINGS

MAIN REEF ROAD

Recovering Gold from Dumps

RECOVERED WATER PIPELINES
TAILINGS SLURRY PIPELINES
GOLD SLURRY PIPELINES   PUMP STATION
PUMP STATION   GOLD TO REFINERY

SAND/SLIME DAMS   GOLD PROCESSING PLANT   TAILINGS DEPOSITION SITES
OTHER PROPERTY OWNERS   MINING LAND

SHAFTS

RECOVERING GOLD FROM DUMPS

CROWN PLANT   CITY DEEP PLANT   RAND REFINERY   KNIGHTS PLANT   ERGO PLANT   DAGGAFONTEIN PLANT

MAIN REEF ROAD

CROWN TAILINGS DEPOSITION SITE   BRACKPAN TAILINGS DEPOSITION SITE   DAGGAFONTEIN TAILINGS DEPOSITION SITE

Thesis Construct Equality

Gold Ecologies

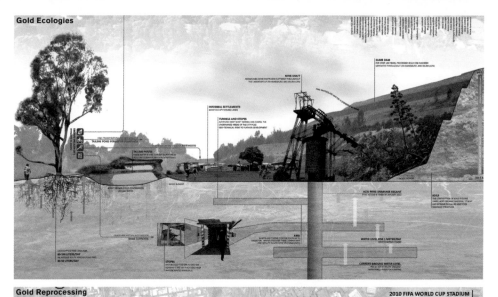

SLIME DAM
FOR OVER 100 YEARS, PROCESSED GOLD ORE HAS BEEN DEPOSITED THROUGHOUT JOHANNESBURG AND SOWETO

MINE SHAFT
ABANDONED MINE SHAFTS ARE SCATTERED THROUGHOUT THE LANDSCAPE OF JOHANNESBURG AND SOWETO

INFORMAL SETTLEMENTS
MANY OCCUPY MINING LANDS

TUNNELS AND STOPES
ACTIVE AND DEEP SHAFT MINING HAS CEASED, THE UNDERMINED AREAS OF THE CITY POSE GEO-TECHNICAL RISKS TO FURTHER DEVELOPMENT

TAILING PONDS
PHASE WATER STORED COLLECTS SLURRY MUD, SOILS, PROCESS WATER FOR ACID MINE DRAINAGE

ACID MINE DRAINAGE DECANT

SOILS
THE COMPOSITION OF SOILS IN SLIME DAMS, LACK ORGANIC MATERIAL. IT IS SILT AND EXTREMELY ALKALIZE MINE RYER DRAINAGE STRUCTURE

AMD
STOPES AND TUNNELS EXPOSE PYRITE TO OXIDATION. WATER DISSOLVES THESE COMPOUNDS AND RESULTS IN ACID MINE DRAINAGE (AMD)

WATER LEVEL RISE 1 METER/DAY

STOPES
WITHIN AND ALONG THE SEAM WAY THE MINE PLACE GOLD MAP WAS EXCAVATED MANUALLY

CURRENT GROUND WATER LEVEL

Gold Reprocessing

2010 FIFA WORLD CUP STADIUM

TAILINGS DISCHARGE

BACKHOE EXCAVATOR
ONE BACKHOE CONSTANTLY BUILDS TAILINGS DEPOSITION

TAILINGS DEPOSITION
FINAL STORAGE OF SLURRY

INFRASTRUCTURE
MINE LANDS FORM A CONTINUOUS STRIP THAT IS PERFECT FOR THE INSERTION OF MODERN INFRASTRUCTURE

CROWN GOLD PROCESSING PLANT
PROCESSES GOLD ORE TO 98% GOLD BARS

SIFTER & WASHING
SECOND SIFTING AND WASHING TO CREATE INITIAL SLURRY

SLURRY PUMP
FINAL ONSITE SIFTING, WASHING, AND SLURRY COMPOSITION CREATION FOR PUMPING LONG DISTANCES

Model

Woodland Remediation

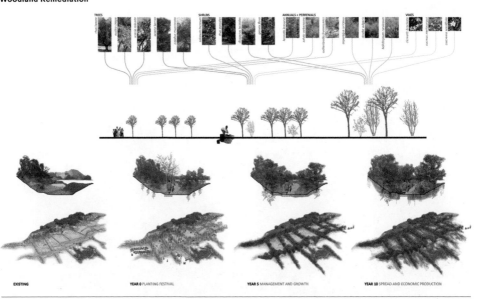

TREES   SHRUBS   ANNUALS + PERRENIALS   VINES

EXISTING   YEAR 0 PLANTING FESTIVAL   YEAR 5 MANAGEMENT AND GROWTH   YEAR 10 SPREAD AND ECONOMIC PRODUCTION

MASS DESIGN GROUP: BUTARO HOSPITAL

STUDENT RESEARCH

PROJECT TEAM
SIERRA BAINBRIDGE, MICHAEL MURPHY, MARIKA SHIOIRI-CLARK, ALAN RICKS, RYAN LEIDNER, GARRET GANTNER, CODY BIRKEY, EBBE STRATHAIRN, NICHOLAS RUTIKANGA, DAVE SALADIK, ALDA LY

Burera District is one of the last two districts in Rwanda to receive a district hospital, and the Butaro hospital will be the first in this region, serving over 400,000 people. Situated on the site of a former military base, Butaro Hospital will serve as both a reminder to and a symbol of Rwanda's incredible transformation since the devastating war of 1994. Using the expertise of infectious disease doctors from Partners in Health and the Harvard Medical School, the Butaro hospital will utilize innovative design solutions through patient flow, and natural ventilation to help mitigate and ultimately reduce the transmission of airborne diseases like Tuberculosis.

Our design uses nearly all local materials—like the volcanic rock from the Virunga Mountain Chain—in an effort to respond to local conditions and stimulate the economy of the Northern Province. Finally, because our client is an NGO committed to serving the poor, our design uses thoughtful financing and material choice to reduce the cost of this hospital to roughly one third of what a hospital of this size should typically cost in Rwanda. MASS, an NGO started by Harvard GSD students in 2006, lead the design process and is currently administrating construction and managing coordination with the all subconsultants, as well as communications with the client.

The city, politically, is the major hope for those of us who are strangers, excluded, marginalized. It is the very stage of democratic causes. The city, as democracy, is something to come. The city wants more effort.

In this way, we all participate in the process of making it.

The question is that this effort requires all kinds of collaboration between many different parties. It requires political passion, freedom to express one's own views, the right to disagree, to dissent, to protest, to study. To remember to be a witness to something that went wrong in order to propose a manifest disagreement, with the hope of reaching a better world. So, testament, mourning.

A monument is not only there to remember, to commemorate but also to give us a warning, a memento. To be aware that something may happen again.

So, do something. With both image of monument as witness but also as oneself as witness. We ourselves are witnesses, and we ourselves should animate the democratic process.

The city must listen to its own silences because the speech of the city, as someone has pointed out, is also the silence of the city.

So for all those who work in its ruins, its shadows, illegal residents, immigrants. The painfully affected families, the abused, the excluded, the survivors, the victims of contemporary slavery, trapped in commercial and industrial abuse. To transmit this kind of city to the city of victims, the city of the vanquished is an important task and must be undertaken by those who know, the free speakers.

XINPENG YU

Negotiate Growth

This section examines the potential for design to responsibly guide urbanization and to address the ecological, social, and spatial problems that accompany steadily increasing global populations. Through large regional strategies and detailed interventions, designers can organize growth, moderate climate change, manage resources, and navigate sustainable futures for growing cities.

SUSTAINABLE MEGA-CITIES

LECTURE | MARCELO EBRARD MAYOR OF MEXICO CITY NOVEMBER 12, 2009, EXCERPT

Let me start by sharing some figures with you. This is Mexico City. The last survey about mobility in the metropolitan zone of Mexico City, tells us that 4,000,000 people are coming each day from nearby localities and municipalities to Mexico City. 4,000,000 each day.

And then, you have the metropolitan area population, which is something around 21,000,000 people right now.

Water consumption in the city. Right now, we are importing thirty-two cubic meters per second to the city, which is one of the most expensive and complex systems on Earth, because we bring the water from a long distance, and then use a very expensive system to dump the water. Vitals: $3,750,000 each day.

Trips per day in the city: More or less, 28,300,000. In 1904, we had ten kilometers per hour as the average speed in the city. In the sixties, the average speed was something like twenty kilometers per hour. But what happens today? We return to eight kilometers.

We need a new vision about what kind of city Mexico City should be in the next 20 years. "What kind of city do we want to have in the next ten or twenty years?" This is the first question.

We started by saying, "How are we going to build a community if we have a city that's very unequal today?" So the first objective in order to build a new vision for the city—in order to really work for our community—is to have equity; to have social facilities for everyone. That's why social development is so important. We have 2,000,000 people in poverty in the city right now, and in the metropolitan zone, maybe twice that. So this is a key issue.

HARVARD UNIVERSITY
GRADUATE SCHOOL OF DESIGN

The other thing related to social development is education. Why education? If you take a look at the Mexican figures about high school, you are going to find out that more or less, more than forty percent of the young people who should be in high schools are on the streets. They don't have opportunities. They are not part of the future of the society.

If we really plan to have sustainability in the long term, this means a change of our behavior and vision in the city.

That's why we are putting a lot of effort into the health systems. We have new systems for how to deal with the health issue in a cheaper way and in a faster way, because if we plan to solve this issue in the old-fashioned way, we should expect something like twenty years to solve the problem, and that is if we even get the money.

The other thing that we are doing with special interests is about science and technology. We are leading a really important effort in order to improve the education in science and technology to be sure that, really, the majority of the people can have access to the new technologies in the city. This is the main task: to improve the connection between the Mexican scientific community and the international one. Next year, we are going to have several forums and congresses in the city with this idea.

And we have the green plan. The green plan is to have a new vision in the city. Natural resources and public space are linked to the green plan, not as an idea isolated from a new vision of the city. Water consumption, transportation facilities, air quality, waste management, energy, and obviously, climate change. We have a climate action program, and our main goal is to reduce more than eleven percent of the total emissions in the city with several measures for mitigation, adaption, and communication actions.

Mobility in the city. Metrobús is the most important initiative in this area, as well as the subways and new systems in the public transportation facilities. And bikes. We are starting a bike station system, similar to Barcelona or Paris or other cities in the world. But also, we are closing important avenues for the people who want to share. For instance, you can have your dog, you have the bike, or you have several options, and we build a community in the no car zone.

If you take a look at other cities in the world, the majority of them are making really important decisions on the climate change issue, but the national governments are behind. It doesn't make sense to make decisions only in the cities, to have goals only in the cities, if they are going to postpone in Copenhagen, again, a serious agreement.

Mexico City is working with other cities in the world in order to present to our national governments and the national authorities the idea to really make urgent decisions and not to postpone again the crucial and most important decisions to the climate change.

FOGGY ARCHITECTURE

OPTION STUDIO   PRESTON SCOTT COHEN

This studio explored the intersection of form and formlessness as an urban and architectural phenomenon. On the one hand, the authorless composite reality of the city, undesigned and unfathomable as a totality, is the envy of contemporary architects seeking liberation from the tired and futile formal devices of design in the face of the larger collective power embodied by the urban scale. On the other hand, there are numerous strategies of architectural production that aim to produce analogous forms of complexity by substituting architectural composition with other processes of design, including computational means, that elude authorial control. The two tendencies, to merge architecture with the city and to conceive its forms by means that thwart conscious design, were made all the more acute by the large city chosen to work on, Chongqing, China, where order is unwieldy, and the buildings are topographically challenged and visually impeded by the nearly ceaseless foggy weather. We assumed these difficult circumstances to pose a particular architectural problem: to reconceive the theme of complexity with computation and to propose typologically and programmatically hybrid buildings, articulated according to the logic of lightweight systems of interior and exterior surface construction compatible with the constraints of the context. Parallel to the form/formless dialectic was an investigation of architectural surface effects of heaviness and lightness, thickness and thinness. A trip to China was planned to include visits to important contemporary architectural case studies in selected cities, exploration of sites in Chongqing, and a tour of one of the leading manufacturers of cladding systems in Changzhou.

Option Studio Negotiate Growth

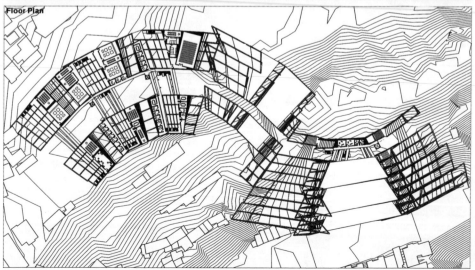

Floor Plan

Floor Plan

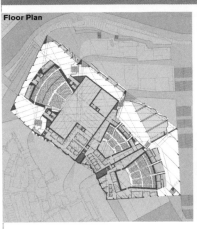

Section

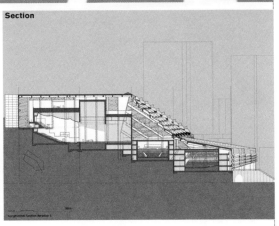

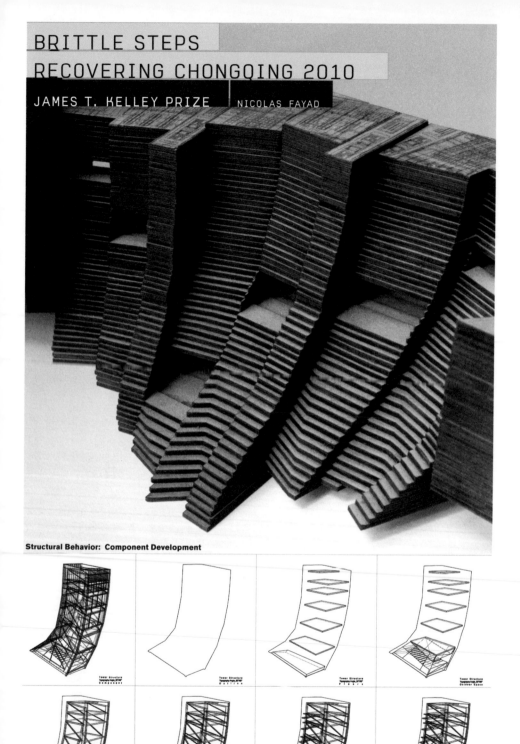

BRITTLE STEPS
RECOVERING CHONGQING 2010

JAMES T. KELLEY PRIZE | NICOLAS FAYAD

Structural Behavior: Component Development

Transversal Section: Prototype Development

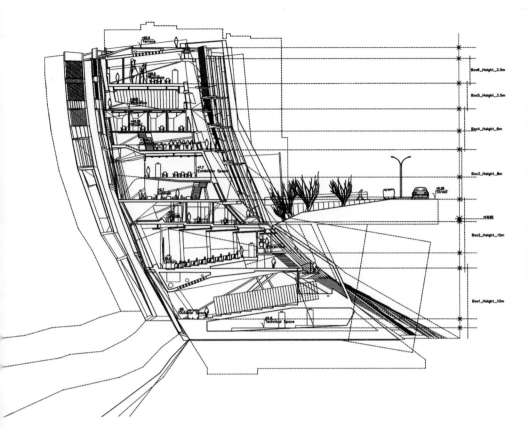

Plan at +10m: Prototype Development

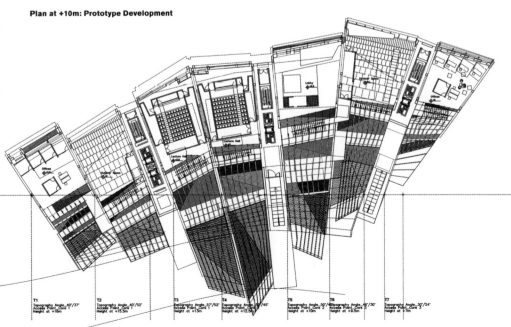

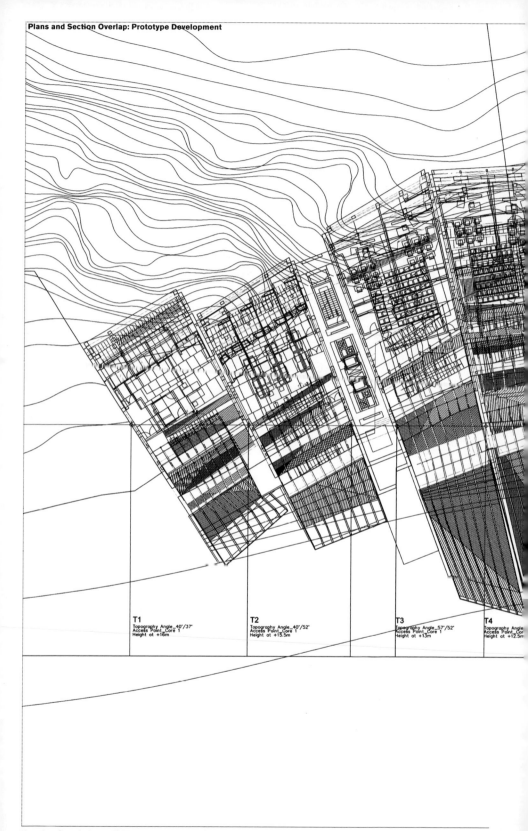

T1
Topography Angle_40°/37°
Access Point_Core 1
Height at +16m

T2
Topography Angle_40°/52°
Access Point_Core 1
Height at +15.5m

T3
Topography Angle_57°/52°
Access Point_Core 1
Height at +13m

T4
Topography Angle
Access Point_Cor
Height at +12.5m

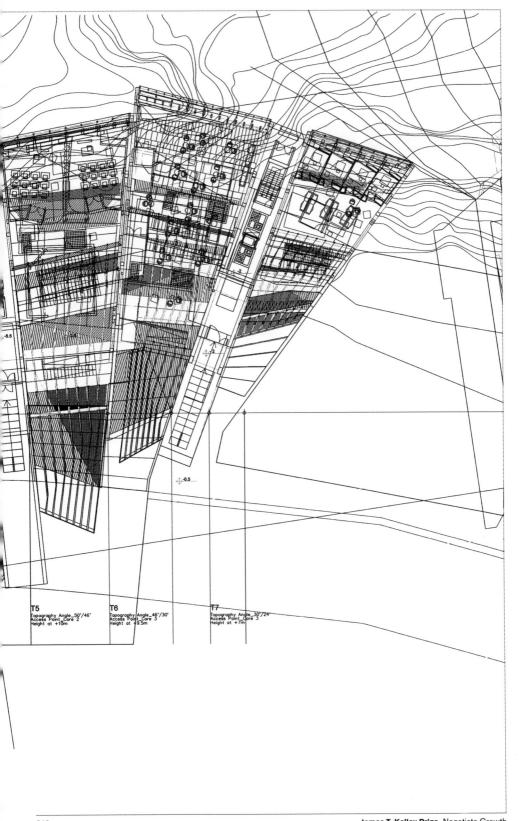

T5
Topography Angle_50°/46°
Access Point_Core 2
Height at +10m

T6
Topography Angle_46°/30°
Access Point_Core 3
Height at +9.5m

T7
Topography Angle_30°/24°
Access Point_Core 3
Height at +7m

LANDSCAPE DISURBANISM: DECENTRALIZATION AND DEPOLDERIZATION IN THE DUTCH DELTA REGION

OPTION STUDIO | PIERRE BELANGER, NINA-MARIE LISTER

Over seventy percent of the GDP in the Netherlands is produced below sea level. To uphold this submergent economy, the Netherlands must spend 2 billion Euros annually on flood defense, equivalent to per capita spending on military defense in the U.S. Notwithstanding dwindling reserves of natural gas in the North Sea, Dutch energy demand—which includes water pumping systems and flood control structures—rely on the import of 976 thousand barrels per day, mostly from the Middle East. To withstand the projected sea level rise between now and the 22d century, flood infrastructure in the Netherlands must be raised 1.3 meters this century and an additional 4 meters following, while groundwater simultaneously drops 1.75 meters. When we talk about climate change and sustainability, what exactly are we trying to sustain? Should we fear sea level rise or exploit it? Should we shore up the Netherlands or let it flood? How do we deal with depleting energy resources and population pressures? Can design and planning preempt challenges that don't yet exist?

The future of the Netherlands is clearly inseparable from the future of energy, engineering, and ecology. Responding to the current call for rearmoring coastal defenses across the Netherlands, this design research project took on the double bind of climate change and urbanization with a design research studio that first addressed the regional challenges of the Maas-Rhine River Delta, a region squeezed in by rising sea levels and increasing flood waters. Examining a series of urban deltas worldwide, the project brought to the surface a series of adaptive flood strategies and disurbanist spatial models—including decentralization, deengineering, and depolderization—that have evolved over centuries to challenge the prevailing polder model and Dutch tradition of civil engineering that have evolved over the past seven hundred years by proposing a series of proto-ecological interventions for the Delta Region that capitalize on the climate conundrum of the 21st century.

Option Studio Negotiate Growth

Building the Terp

I operate a dredger for Boskalis. I transport contaminated dredge from the Biesbosch to Dordrecht for remediation. I like it because it is nearby and accessible.

They've offered me a fair price for my farm, or a plot on the terp. Still, it's hard to imagine flooding this land, I've worked for a long time to keep it dry. But they say its for the best, and maybe my children will want to stay if we have land in the new town.

A gradual, vegetated littoral zone will promote biological soil cohesion, effectively reducing soil erosion without the use of engineered surfaces and slopes. Agents in this process include bio-membranes, mollusc armouring, roots, and exopolymers.

I work at the short rotational forest. We cut and grind the willows for use as biofuel. We also take cuttings for propagation in new plots or as bundles for reed establishment.

Many native, flood species can be used for slope stabiliza Betula pendula

reed houses

willow harvest

reed harvest

| depoldered fields as intertidal zone | average winter high water line | storm floodplain (1-10 yr flood gradient) | existing dike | dre |

Building the Terp

The process of gradient urbanism begins with site preparation to enable inundation of strategically selected polders. Because most polders are situated above low-tide water level the first step will be to excavate channels to create passages for water during low-flow periods harvest as a building material. Next, the dikes perpendicular to the river will be removed allowing water to enter the polder. Gradually, dredge from nearby waterways will be added to the dikes and remediated incrementally to expand the mound horizontally and vertically. Th flexible; however, "vertical zoning" will provide the basic guidelines for appropriate land-covers. Terp construction will create several specialized industries such as research and monitoring of vegetal systems, aggregate brokers and transporter, and bio-fuel cultivation. harves

Dynamic Normaal Amsterdam Peil d(NAP)

KIMBERLY GARZA, SARAH THOMAS

JAMES MOORE, EAMONN HUTTON

poplars and other ... ... will stabilize the soil and in dewatering and phyto-remediation.

I own the first business to buy land on the terp. We specialize in aggregate broker-ing. We receive, sort and stockpile materi-als from numerous sources. Our products in-clude: sand, gravel, clay, dewatered dredge, crushed concrete, compost and topsoil.

I operate a shipping company in Dusseldorf. We often use construc-tion waste as ballast on our way to Rotterdam. We can sell the material to a broker in Dordrecht before collecting our cargo from the iron.

I'm a student from TU Delft. For my thesis I am studying the survival rates and efficacy of various species of reeds. I hope my study will posi-tion me as an expert for future reed planting projects.

I operate an earthworks company in Dordrecht. We won the contract to prepare the polders for inundation. They say that there are going to be more super terps. We are hoping that our performance here will get us future contracts building terps.

upper elevation +4.0m NAP

lower elevation +2.8m NAP = 1000 yr flood

depoldering process

channel construction
10m x 66m channels excavated prior to opening the dikes. This will produce 33.3 m3 of soil, clay and sand per linear meter of channel. The channel profile is determined by the angle of repose of the building material.

wet clay   15°

initial settlement

aggregate broker

settling pond for dredge effluent

digging canals

digging channel

unbroken dike

bundles of willows used to create protected cells for reed establishment

planting reeds

...ill be used to create a network of dredge storage cells along a selected dike. This will serve as the foundation for terps. During this time, and immediately prior to inundation, the remaining polder plain will be planted with reeds that will ultimately increase sedimentation for ...e 820,000 m3/year, which is enough to create approximately 20 hectares of elevated land per year. The dimensions of the initial terp are based on basic spatial requirements of the infrastructures that will colonize it at first. The rate and form of expansion thereafter will be ...w on current sectors such as earthwork contractors and dredgers. This economy would expand with the terps and eventually migrate to develop more landforms throughout the delta.

Flexible Urbanism

LACI VIDEMSKY, CASEY ELMER

The New Map of Dordrecht

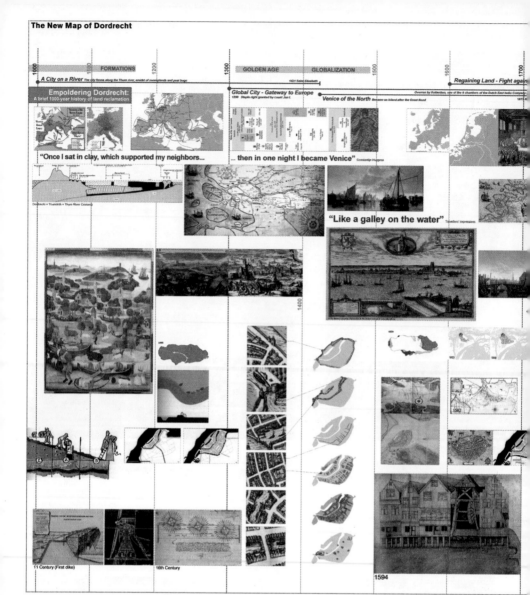

FORMATIONS | GOLDEN AGE | GLOBALIZATION

A City on a River The city forms along the Thure river, amidst of sweetlands and peat bogs. 1421 Saint Elizabeth

Regaining Land - Fight again

Empoldering Dordrecht:
A brief 1000-year history of land reclamation

Global City - Gateway to Europe 1290 Staple right granted by Count Jan I.

Venice of the North Became an island after the Great flood

Overrun by Rotterdam, one of the 6 chambers of the Dutch East India Company

"Once I sat in clay, which supported my neighbors...   ... then in one night I became Venice" Constantijn Huygens

"Like a galley on the water" Travellers' impressions

11 Century (First dike)   16th Century

1594

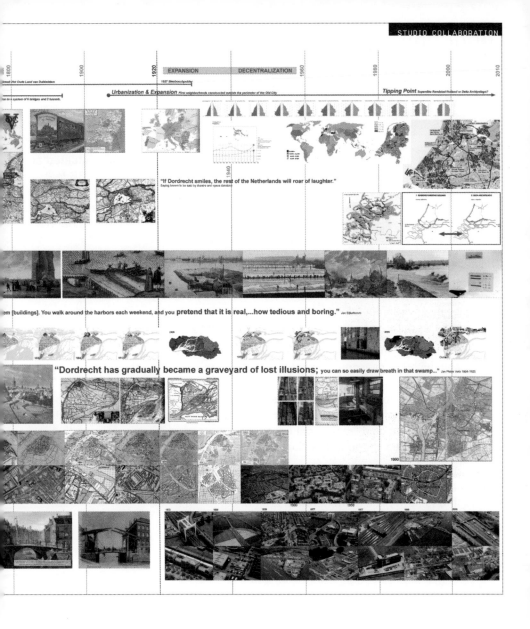

Iquitos, Peru is the largest city in the world that is inaccessible by road. Situated at the source of the Amazon River, the waters surrounding the city fluctuate 30 feet over the course of the year, turning the city from a peninsula to an island annually. This constant and radical transformation of the city's boundary has left the edge tattered and informal, taken over by networks of floating slums, decommissioned infrastructure, ad hoc docks, fishing vessels, and oil rigs.

This thesis is a proposal for a new strategy for the edge of Iquitos and a new entry to the city. The typology of "the Gates of the City" by their functional, ceremonial and iconic presence, invoke architecture's disciplinary motivations. The city of Iquitos by its environmental, economic, social, and post-colonial legacies, defies architecture's posture of permanence and iconography.

In order to address this fluctuating boundary, architecture must be put into a relationship with the moving datum of the water. In this way, this thesis provides an opportunity to challenge the function of form in effecting programmatic, infrastructural and social transformations in relation to this constantly changing ground. As a point of departure the thesis considers the intersection of the water and the architecture as a "reciprocal figure"—like a stone and its ripple—one that is shaped by and gives shape to the site around it.

"Grounds for Architecture" is an attempt to investigate the feedback loop between architecture and site, through a close investigation of form. Therefore, both the resultant form as well as its generation are critical to the thesis.

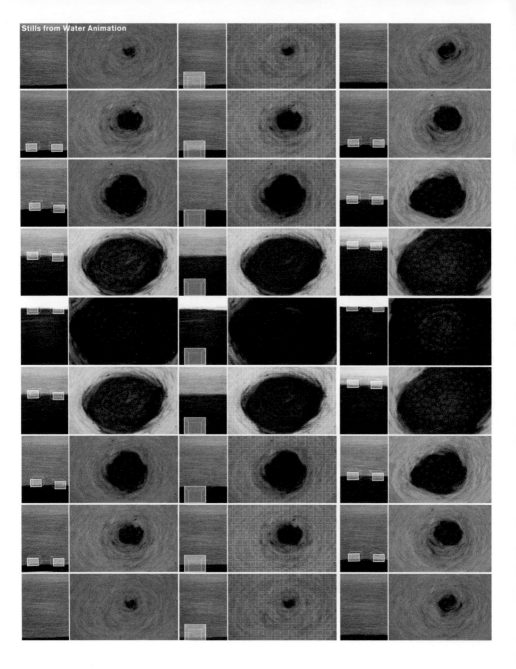

Stills from Water Animation

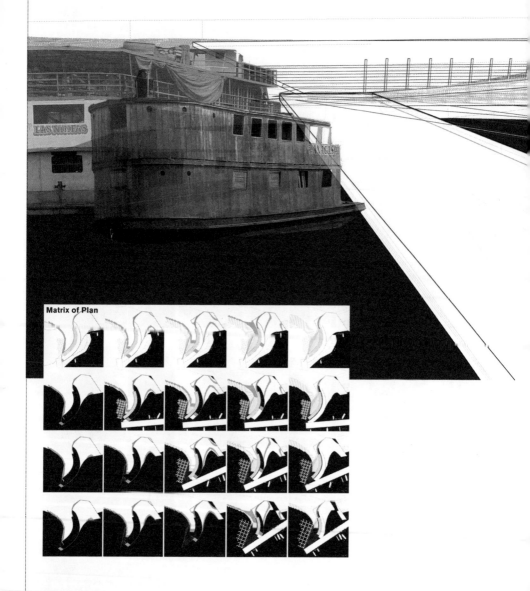

Matrix of Plan

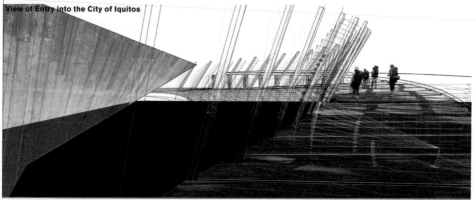

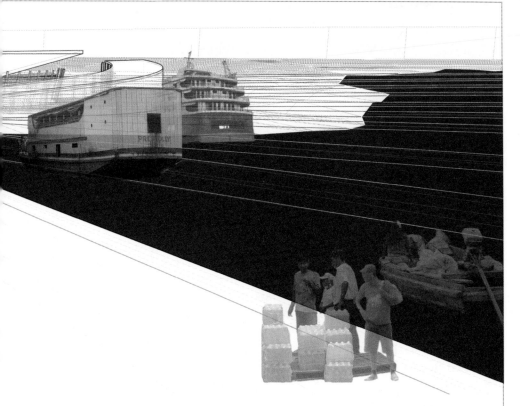

Conceptual Diagrams

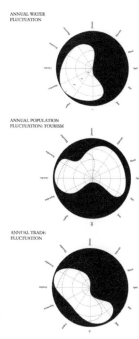

ANNUAL WATER
FLUCTUATION

ANNUAL POPULATION
FLUCTUATION: TOURISM

ANNUAL TRADE
FLUCTUATION

ARCHITECTURE III

CORE | INSTRUCTORS: JONATHAN LEVI, NATHANIEL BELCHER, JOHN HONG, TIMOTHY HYDE, MARIANA IBANEZ, FLORIAN IDENBURG | FALL 2009

The third of a four-semester sequence of design studios brought together the exploration of /type/ with the technique of architectural form-making. The studio vehicle was a precinct of university housing including a mixture of academic components. Housing typologies were explored within the context of the overall university project, considering programmatic relationships between individuals and groups that support knowledge creation and intellectual discourse. The semester-long project was subdivided into a series of focus studies targeting the formal, spatial, and technical development of the full spectrum of scales from that of human occupation to the aggregation of units and the shaping of interior and exterior public spaces.

The purpose of this studio was to study housing through the vehicle of the institutional question that is raised by the addition of new housing to the existing Harvard campus fabric. We looked at housing from the finest scale of human occupation to the arrangement of groupings in relation to the organization of campus and city. We considered the individual and the grouping of individuals in relation to the institutional mission of intellectual exchange.

The specific project was the creation of new academic housing to be located within two study areas in and around campus. The housing may be in the form of a separate 13th house or strategic additions to existing houses. An undergraduate house is both housing and an admixture of academic, cultural, social, and athletic components. Our goal was to espouse models of physical planning that provide for the future—not just the present or the past.

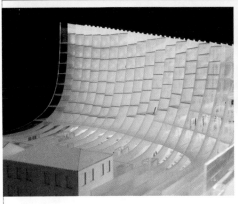

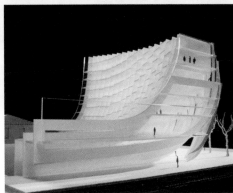

Formal Logic Diagram

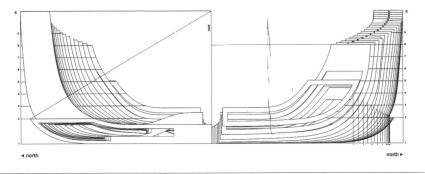

◄ north

north ►

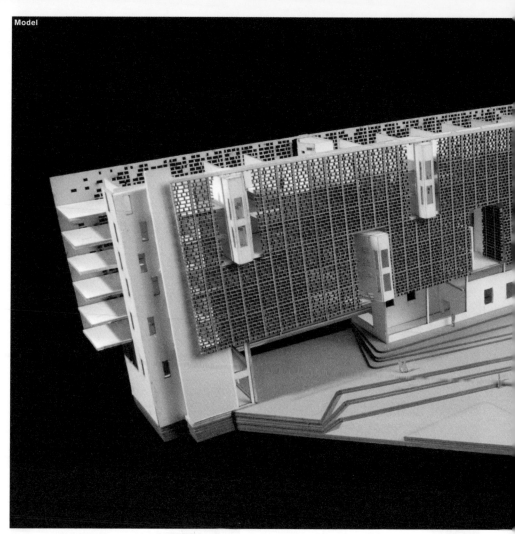

Model

West Sectional Elevation

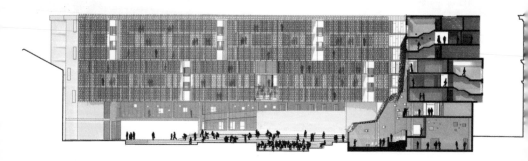

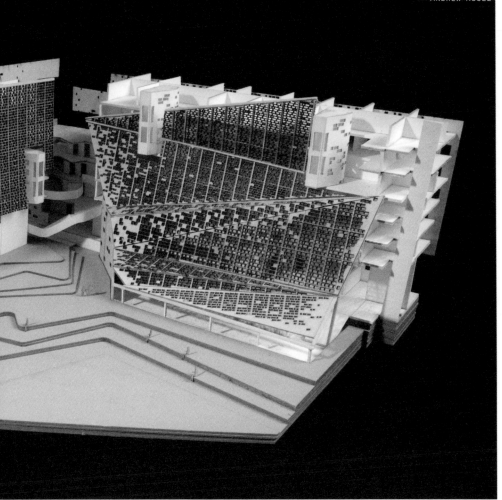

Ground Floor Plan

Exterior Approach from South

JESSICA VAUGHN

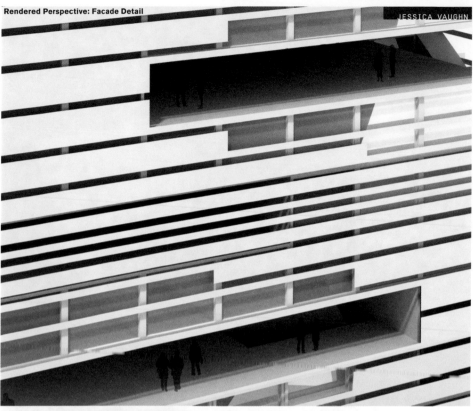

Unit Aggregation: Sectional View

MATTHEW WAXMAN

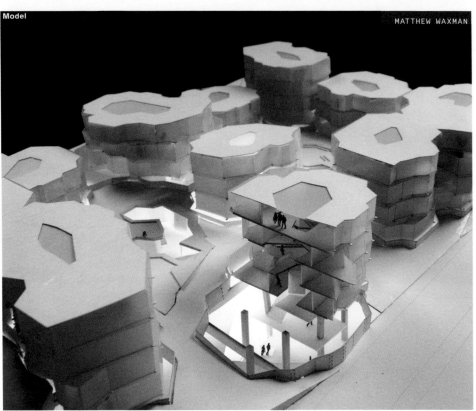

Roofscape Plan with Interior Plans of Housing Towers

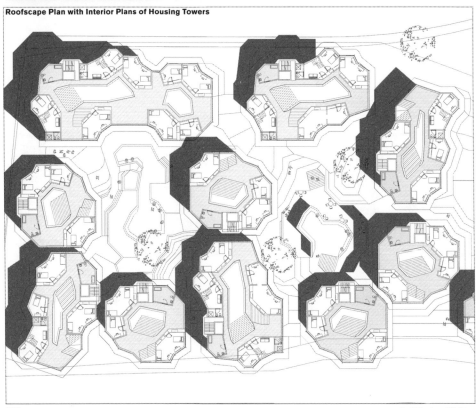

Ground Level Entrance and Housing Above

STEPHANIE LIN

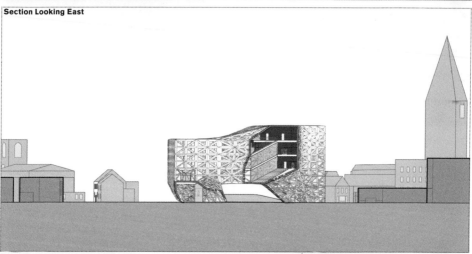

Section Looking East

View of Lobby, Theater and Circulation to Housing

Exterior Night Rendering

PAUL MERRILL

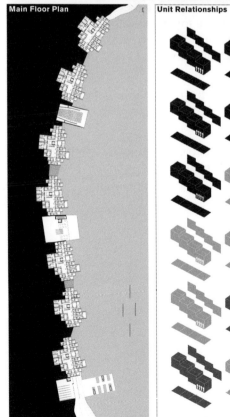

Main Floor Plan

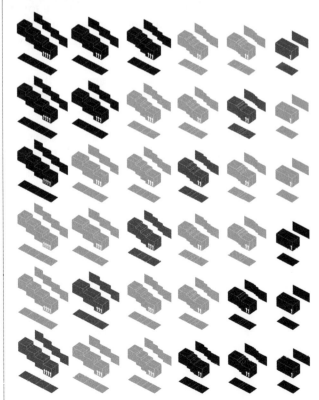

Unit Relationships

LANDSCAPE ARCHITECTURE III

CORE INSTRUCTORS: CHRISTIAN WERTHMANN, PIERRE BELANGER, JANE HUTTON, PAUL COTE SPRING 2010

This course reinforced and built upon the range of conventions of landscape architectural production introduced in previous core studios and academic courses. Emphasis was placed on precision and craft in conceptual, schematic, and design development abilities. Issues of the physical, socioeconomic, technological, architectural, and ideological forces underlying the organization and form of human communities were incorporated into a series of projects. These ranged from the complex reading and mapping of the city, the development and testing of innovative program strategies in unconventional sites, and the development of design ideas to the advanced schematic stage. At each stage, students were expected to reconcile the sometimes-conflicting characteristics among land resources, development pressures, privacy, and commonality. Throughout, a strong reciprocity between depth of thinking and the act of making was sought.

Objectives:

1. To gain a critical understanding of the issues, influences, and generative possibilities in landscape design and planning within the contemporary urban environment.

2. To provide a bridge between the concerns of landscape theory and individual design practices. The need for a theoretical basis for action within the shifting and complex nature of the communities we form and inhabit were explored. Investigations of the nature, meaning, and social role of public and private spatial orders were examined.

3. To identify concerns for human settlement within the dynamics of urban ecology. The processes of growth, transformation, and the complex layering of ownership, density, distribution, and territoriality were explored.

4. To develop and refine both analytical and analogical skills in the interpretation, representation, and production of landscape architectural design and planning.

AMY LINNE, FORBES LIPSCHITZ, XIAOXUAN LU

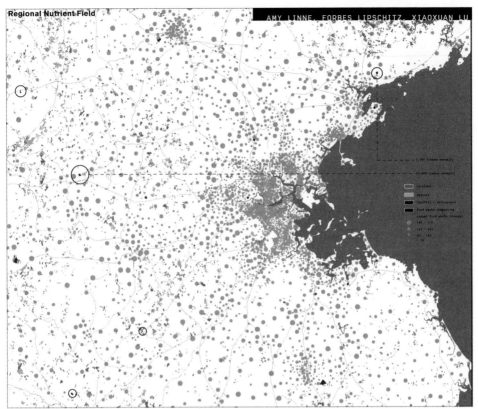

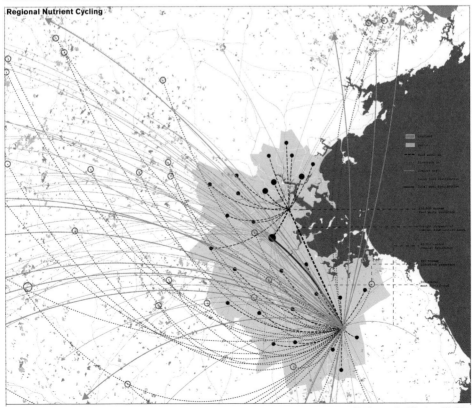

Regional Nutrient Cycling

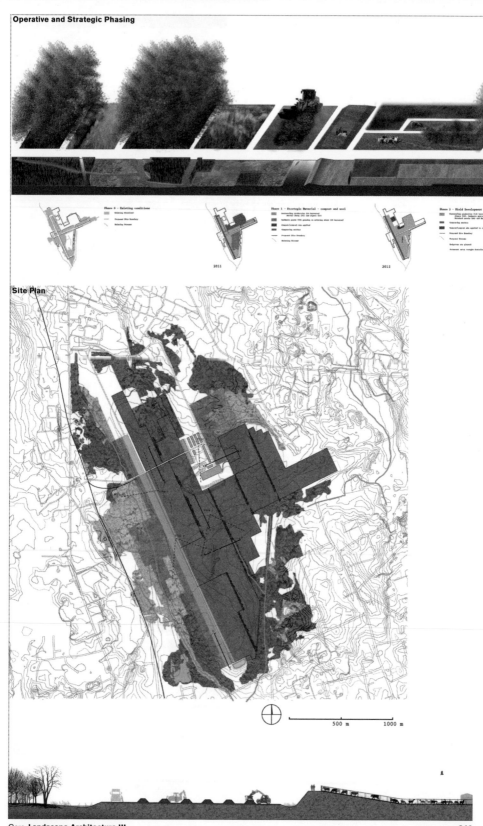

Operative and Strategic Phasing

Phase 0 - Existing conditions

Phase 1 - Strategic Material - compost and soil

Phase 2 - Field Development - capping w

2011

2012

Site Plan

500 m   1000 m

AMY LINNE, FORBES LIPSCHITZ, XIAOXUAN LU

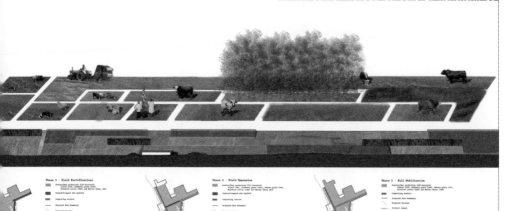

Phase 3 - Field Fortifications

2014

Phase 4 - Field Expansion

2015

Phase 5 - Full Mobilization

Site Renderings

Perspective: Maximum Energy Generation

Potential Energy Build-Out Scenarios for 2050

Land Use Types and Widths

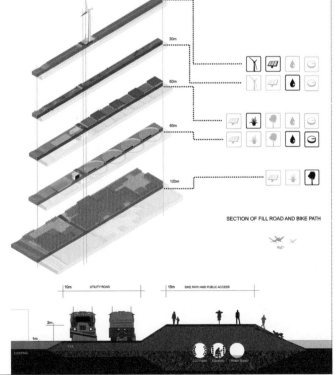

SECTION OF FILL ROAD AND BIKE PATH

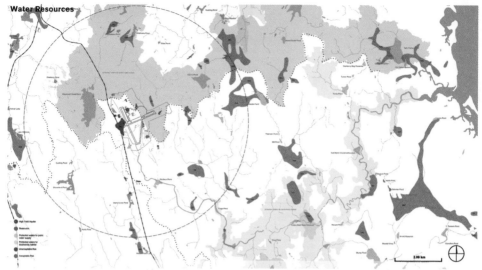

Water Resources

Tri-Town Water

Terminal Perspective

YENLIN CHENG, R. CHARLES HOWE, LI SUN

Strategic Timeline

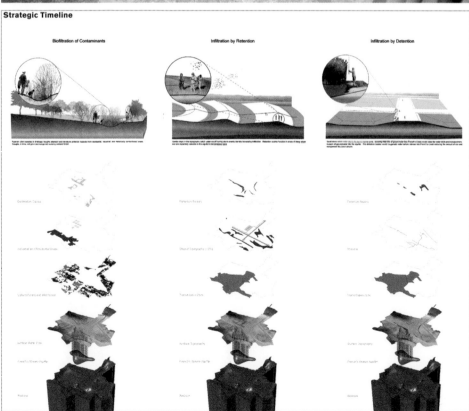

ELEMENTS OF URBAN DESIGN

CORE   INSTRUCTORS: FELIPE CORREA, ANITA BERRIZBEITIA, RAFAEL SEGAL   FALL 2009

Elements of Urban Design was an advanced core studio for the post professional programs in urban design. The studio introduced a wide host of ideas, strategies, and technical skills associated with current thinking on urbanism, and speculated on the designer's projective role in analyzing and shaping complex metropolitan systems. Rigorous research informed a series of interrelated exercises that construct diverse hypotheses about new formal and experiential urban identities across multiple scales of intervention and development. For the Fall 2009 semester, this core studio focused on The Grand Concourse and Boulevard in the Bronx, NY.

Analysis of the Present Condition of the Edge

ANGEL RODRIGUEZ COLON

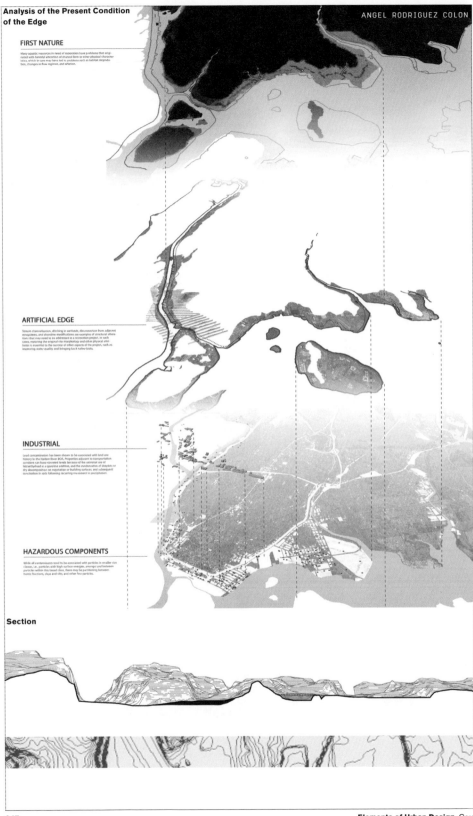

FIRST NATURE

Many aquatic resources in need of restoration have problems that originated with harmful alteration of channel form or other physical characteristics, which in turn may have led to problems such as habitat degradation, changes in flow regimes, and siltation.

ARTIFICIAL EDGE

Stream channelization, ditching in wetlands, disconnection from adjacent ecosystems, and shoreline modifications are examples of structural alterations that may need to be addressed in a restoration project. In such cases, restoring the original site morphology and other physical attributes is essential to the success of other aspects of the project, such as improving water quality and bringing back native biota.

INDUSTRIAL

Lead contamination has been shown to be associated with land use history in the Harlem River BOA. Properties adjacent to transportation corridors can have elevated levels because of the universal use of tetraethyllead as a gasoline additive, and the condensation of droplets or dry decomposition on vegetation or building surfaces, and subsequent constitution in soils following recurring movement in precipitation.

HAZARDOUS COMPONENTS

While all contaminants tend to be associated with particles in smaller size classes, i.e., particles with high surface energies amongst and between particles within this broad class, there may be partitioning between humic fractions, clays and silts, and other fine particles.

Section

HSIAO ROU HUANG, HUNGKAI LIAO

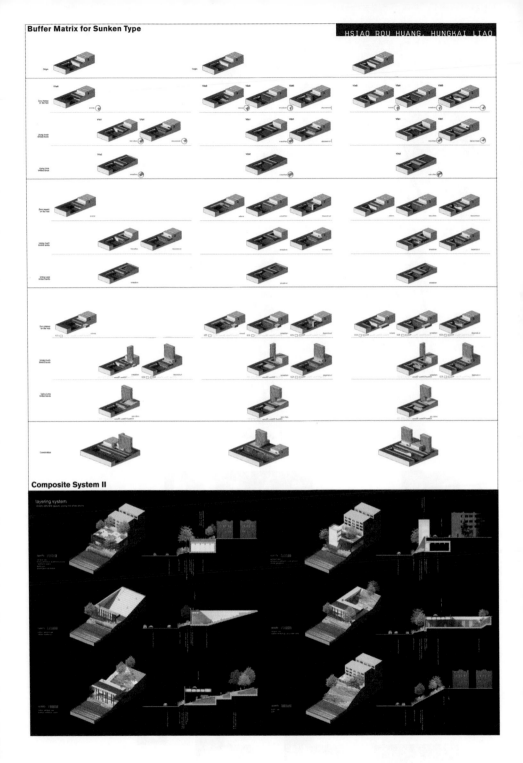

Composite System II

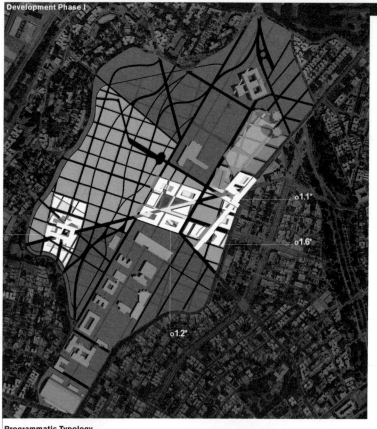

Programmatic Typology

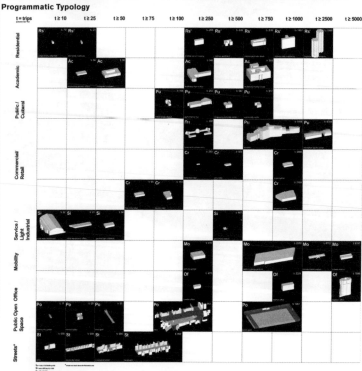

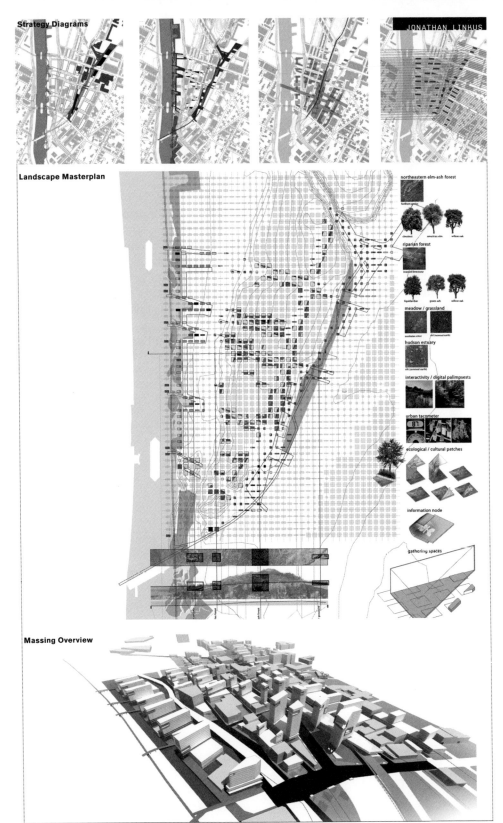

Strategy Diagrams

JONATHAN LINKUS

Landscape Masterplan

northeastern elm-ash forest

riparian forest

meadow / grassland

hudson estuary

interactivity / digital palimpsests

urban tacometer

ecological / cultural patches

information node

gathering spaces

Massing Overview

Elements of Urban Design Core

SUSTAINABILITY
FOR PLANNING AND DESIGN

SEMINAR   CHRISTIAN WERTHMANN
FEATURED SPEAKERS
PETER DEL TREDICI, RICHARD T.T. FORMAN, SANFORD KWINTER, MOHSEN MOSTAFAVI,
CHRISTOPH REINHART, PETER ROSE, HASHIM SARKIS, DANIEL SCHRAG,
THOMAS SCHROEPFER, MATTHIAS SCHULER, CHARLES WALDHEIM,
CHRISTIAN WERTHMANN

This survey course established basic environmental literacy for all the departments at the school. A series of lecturers addressed key issues for planners and designers connected to the term sustainability. The lectures specifically addressed the many scales of design and planning by discussing the chosen topics from a local, regional, national, and global perspective revealing the interdependence between architecture, landscape architecture, urban design, and urban planning. Starting out with a foundation session on theory, later lectures discussed the latest thinking on topics such as ecology and biodiversity, climate change, energy, water, soils and plants, mobility, microclimate, light and materials. The series finished with a critical discussion of current examples of environmental urbanism.

Hans Carl von Carlowitz, inventor of the term
Nachhaltigkeit (Sustainability)

Sylvicultura Oeconomica,
by Hans Carl von Carlowitz, 1713

DAYLIGHTING NOMOGRAPHS REVISITED

MDESS THESIS | ROHIT MANUDHANE

ADVISOR: CHRISTOPH REINHART

This study presents a critical review of a classic 1984 paper titled "LBL Daylighting Nomographs," written by Selkowitz and Gabel using RADIANCE/DAYSIM simulations combined with the light switch occupant behavior model. In this study an attempt is made to reproduce some of the older nomograph in RADIANCE/DAYSIM and review their applicability in the light of recent knowledge related to occupant use of manual shading and lighting controls. The initial step of the study is to reproduce the DOE2 simulations that were used to establish the original nomographs with RADIANCE based annual DAYSIM simulations, using the exact same assumptions for occupant use of personal controls as in the original paper. We then apply current knowledge on occupant behavior to predict how energy savings from the use of photo-sensor controlled dimming systems vary compared to the early prediction method. This hypothesis was tested for an example of a medium sized side-lit office building located in Boston, and the resultant comparison showed that the new more realistic nomographs would predict about 25% less energy savings than the old nomographs.

Blinds can make a significant impact on the lighting energy consumption patterns within buildings

Comparative results of Scenarios 1, 2 & 3

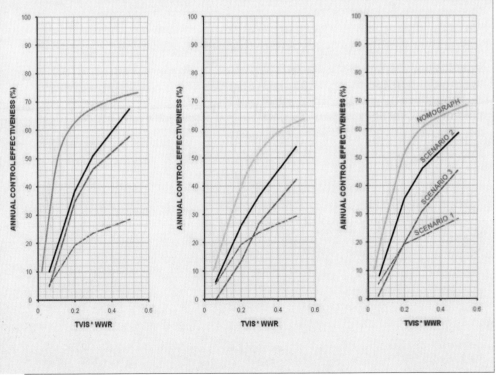

LANDSCAPE AND ECOLOGICAL URBANISM: ALTERNATIVES FOR BEIJING CITY NORTHWEST

OPTION STUDIO KONGJIAN YU, JANE HUTTON, STEPHEN ERVIN

Beijing, China is one of the fastest developing regions in the world and among the most challenging places for the study and practice of urbanism and landscape architecture. In the past 30 years, the area of the city has expanded 700%, the population has doubled to 17 million, and both population and land consumption will continue to expand. As development continues, pressing challenges include: rapid environmental degradation, severe water shortages and pollution, crippling transportation and mobility restrictions, and the loss of cultural identity. The studio focused on alternative futures for Sujiatuo, a township in the hilly urban fringe of Northwest Beijing, that is under severe development pressure because of rapid urbanization in the surrounding region. Sujiatuo, composed of several villages and covering an area of 100 km², is famous for its beautiful landscape, unique cultural heritage, and rich biodiversity. While 300,000 people inhabit the basin terrain in Sujiatuo, development is only now expanding up the mountainsides. This development must address the site's complex conditions that include a critical aquifer recharge zone, sensitive biophysical systems, large-scale climatic issues, as well as economic development and the future of the agricultural communities that live there. As development is inevitable, the questions of "What kinds of development should occur?", "How do we maintain the area's culture and heritage?", and "Where and how can we balance development and conservation?" become the main concerns of the municipal and local governments.

The aims of this studio were to develop urban and landscape strategies for the region based on analysis of the ecological and socio-economic context, and to develop alternative landscape and urban design proposals at a site-scale that respond to regional development scenarios. The studio emphasized regional scale planning and the resolution of design proposals at a fine scale.

Integrated Seasonal River Park

ROBERT DE MIGUEL, DIANE LIPOVSKY

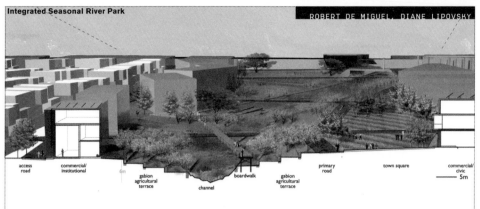

access road   commercial/ institutional   gabion agricultural terrace   channel   boardwalk   gabion agricultural terrace   primary road   town square   commercial/ civic

— 5m

R+D Landscape

Regional Plan

Phasing

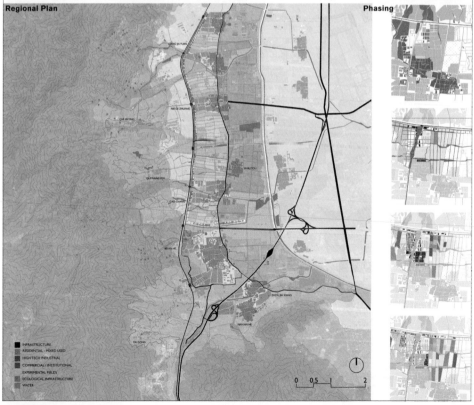

INFRASTRUCTURE
RESIDENTIAL - MIXED USED
HIGHTECH INDUSTRIAL
COMMERCIAL INSTITUTIONAL
EXPERIMENTAL FIELDS
ECOLOGICAL INFRASTRUCTURE
WATER

0   0.5   1   2

Negotiate Growth **Option Studio**

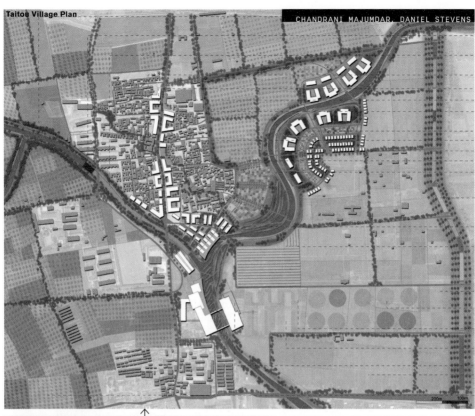

Taitou Village Plan

CHANDRANI MAJUMDAR, DANIEL STEVENS

200m 100m

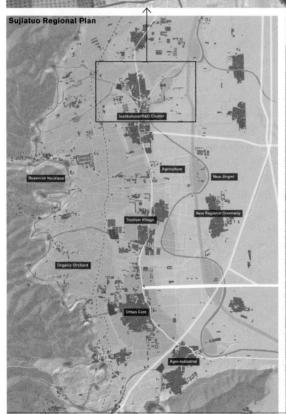

Sujiatuo Regional Plan

Institutional/R&D Cluster

Reservoir Necklace

Agriculture

New Jingmi

Tourism Village

New Regional Greenway

Organic Orchard

Urban Core

Agro-Industrial

Community Agriculture

Option Studio Negotiate Growth

GEOGRAPHIES OF ENERGY: THE CASE OF THE TRANS-ARABIAN PIPELINE

DDES THESIS | RANIA GHOSN

ADVISOR: HASHIM SARKIS

Rania's dissertation has helped define a whole new area of research and inquiry on the landscapes of energy. While expanding our knowledge of the history of oil transportation in the Middle East, her dissertation has also engaged in some of the central theoretical debates about space, technology, and society and emerged with a new theoretical framework, exposing the spatial underpinnings of energy. Along with the New Geographies issue on Landscapes of Energy that Rania edited, her dissertation provides a reference and solid ground for the emergence of a new interdisciplinary domain.

—Hashim Sarkis

Industrial energy systems require space to produce value while keeping at bay the geographic imperative and spatial repercussions of their operation. In the oil system, the international crude pipeline has allowed the control over a region's production through the exclusive ownership of the circulation channel that connects the wells to the terminal port. Although geographies of transport are central to oil, the spatial deployment of the industry's channels has often been dismissed in favor of a smooth "space of flows" and binary accounts of pipe-wars and pipe-dreams.

This dissertation explores the geographies of the Trans-Arabian Pipeline (Tapline), a cross-border line that transported between 1950 and 1975 Aramco crude from the wells of its sister concession in eastern Saudi Arabia, through Jordan and Syria, to a Lebanese port on the Mediterranean. Through the historical case study of the Tapline, I argue that territorial organization is simultaneously a force of production and the space in which frictions over production unfold. Particularly in relation to its convention agreement with Saudi Arabia, and as the boundaries of the sister Aramco concession corresponded with that of the Kingdom, Tapline extended infrastructural provisions in relation to the Kingdom's aspirations to settle, secure, and develop its northern boundary. The pipeline's large-scale technological system materialized a territory with its qualities and frictions opening a space— simultaneously epistemological and geographical—that could be incorporated into forms of political rationalities.

Through the case study of Tapline, Geographies of Energy seeks to spatialize the deployment of energy, map some of the physical, social, and representational geographies of oil transport in particular, and analyze the spatial and socio-ecological transformations in landscapes and livelihoods that occurred as places were incorporated into systems of energy.

WATER, GREENERY, AND A BEAUTIFUL FACE: AN ETHNOGRAPHY OF GREEN IN BAHRAIN

DDES THESIS | GARETH DOHERTY

ADVISOR: HASHIM SARKIS

Gareth has very convincingly argued that the practice of greening desert areas in the Gulf region is not green at all and that it is driven by a series of professional and cultural biases that need to be unpacked. By combining the visual and physical analytic tools of landscape architecture with the ethnographic tools of anthropology, and by focusing his studies on the recent urban development of Bahrain, he proposes a more in-depth reading of how urban practices and aesthetic values are developed and received in contemporary architectural and urban practices. The color (and ethos) green will not be the same again.

—Hashim Sarkis

To have green in urban environments is often not very green from an environmental point of view. In fact, the provision of greenery in most urban areas, with few exceptions, bears significant environmental costs. To be and to have green is mostly presented as a moral imperative, yet the provision of urban greenery is morally questionable, especially in arid environments like Bahrain. This paradox is at the heart of the dissertation: how to manage the obsession with greenery in the urban built environment and design and plan with green in urban areas in a way that is greener, i.e. more environmentally, culturally, politically, and socially sensitive than is generally the case today.

Based on a year of ethnographic fieldwork, the dissertation unpacks some of the concepts of green in the exaggerated condition of Bahrain, proportionately the smallest, densest, and greenest of the Arab states of the Persian Gulf. There, green provides a luscious, albeit expensive, contrast with the arid whites and browns and yellows of the desert. The biggest change that can be made to the desert, as with the city, is to green it.

Positioned in the emerging field of design anthropology, the dissertation makes the case for more nuanced ethnographic methods as a tool for generating and writing about design. Through the focus on green, the dissertation explores the underexplored role of color in discussions of the city.

CITIES IN AN URBAN AGE: DOES DESIGN MATTER?

LECTURE   RICKY BURDETT   OCTOBER 20, 2009. EXCERPT

I've entitled this talk slightly provocatively: "Understanding Cities in a Global Age: Does Design Matter?" To actually ask that question here at the Graduate School of Design is a bit risky, but I think one has to ask that question and remind ourselves that the making of the physical fabric, the creation of quality, has massive impacts on people's lives and on the environmental agenda.

But, what constitutes design? Does actually designing a governance system constitute a piece of design that an architect or an urbanist should be involved in? The answer is absolutely yes. Does designing a transit system go outside the bounds of an architect or an urban designer? Absolutely no. It's something that is totally endemic to the making of sustainable and livable cities.

I think it's important to remind ourselves of where we are in time, not just because two years ago, the United Nations confirmed that half the world's population is living in cities, but just to look back and look forward. The trend, if it continues the way it is—and in fact, it's very likely to exceed it—is that in forty years' time, when my son will be just a little bit older than I am, we will have three quarters of the world's population living in cities.

The question for all of us is, "What is the shape of this? What are we actually doing in terms of design? How are we making it and how are we governing that space to make it, in many ways, more sustainable?"

If there are two things that I would like to leave with you to provide a context to what I'm talking about, they are these two very simple statistics. One has to do with the social and the other one has to do with the environmental. A third of people today who live in cities live in slums of one sort or another. If seventy-five percent of the world's population is going to move into cities in the next thirty or forty years and that number remains the same, it is a massive number that few of us can imagine what that means. And the second key issue is that seventy-five percent of world energy is consumed one way: by buildings and transport associated with cities. And therefore, seventy-five percent of CO_2 emissions are effected by cities. So a small impact on these numbers will make an enormous difference, and I guess the key argument is that design is part of that discussion.

If, as I contend, design is central to the creation of social sustainability in cities and of creating social equity, this image probably summarizes it better than anything else. What you see here are the favelas in São Paulo of Paraisópolis, which has been there for thirty or forty years. It has its own dynamics, but it lacks two things: basic water and basic forms of sewage. When it rains, the place floods and some of the streets disappear. On the right, behind this wall is a recent tower block where the wealth of the individuals here means that each terrace has a swimming pool. It's that level of distinction. It would be naïve to sit here and say that this is unacceptable that two worlds like this actually clash with each other. All cities—particularly in cities where there's a growing economy—will always face this sort of conflict between the two, but not all cities need to create a wall so that even when this group of people raises up in terms of their aspirations and status, they will never be able to connect with what is on the right-hand side. So in many ways, I think the design of the potential connectivity between the left- and the right-hand part of the side is what I want to talk about.

That image I've just showed you of São Paulo summarizes the social exclusion argument. On the environmental side, perhaps Mexico City best illustrates one of our greatest problems today. When this picture was taken only a few years ago, the city happened to end over here. We are about twenty-five miles away from the city center. The distance you need to travel through these areas to actually get to work may be anything between three and four hours if you take a bus. This is a city that today still has 700 or 800 new cars on the roads every day, and it's continuing to sprawl.

What we are talking about doesn't just apply to the favelas of Rio; it doesn't just apply to the emerging cities of the Asian subcontinent, but some of the core themes apply to the decisions we're taking today as planners and civic leaders.

We are reminded that cities exist for very, very simple reasons. They are about the flows of capital, of people, and of goods. Ultimately, the connections between cities will always mean that they will continue to grow.

People will continue to come to cities to get jobs. People will continue to come to cities in order to interact with each other.

Design needs not only to cope with a problem of how to deal with a large quantity but also the speed of change. This slide shows the numbers of people moving into various cities, like Lagos, like Mumbai, and like Dhaka, not per day but per hour. For every minute that I speak, one new person has moved into Lagos.

If Mumbai continues to grow like this, it will continue and overtake Tokyo, which today is the largest city in the world at 36,000,000. The question for us is, "If Mumbai continues to grow in the state that it is now, with half of its population without sewers or water, and in twenty or thirty years, it becomes a city with—whatever it is—35,000,000 people, what sort of condition are we actually creating for the next generation of urban dwellers?"

Now, in terms of design and in terms of understanding of the relationship between the physical and the social, the question becomes, "What is happening as these cities grow? What is happening to the spaces that we create and to the people who inhabit the spaces that are created by the design community across the world?"

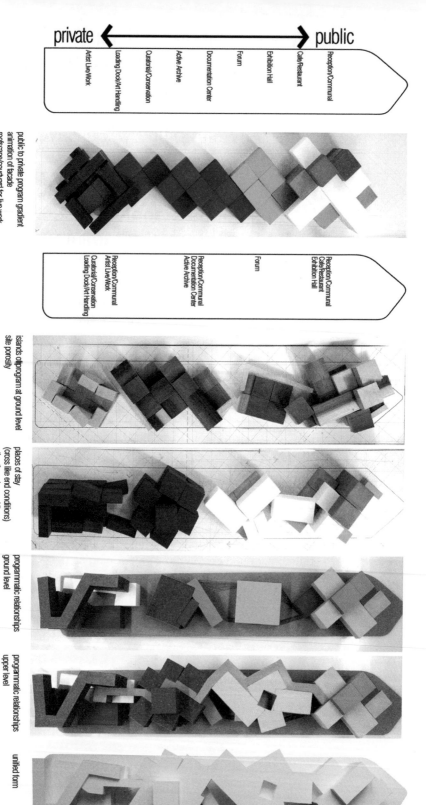

private ← → public

Artist Live/Work
Loading Dock/Art Handling
Curatorial/Conservation
Active Archive
Documentation Center
Forum
Exhibition Hall
Cafe/Restaurant
Reception/Communal

public to private program gradient
animation of facade
roofscape/courtyard for live work

Curatorial/Conservation
Artist Live/Work
Loading Dock/Art Handling

Reception/Communal
Documentation Center
Active Archive

Forum

Reception/Communal
Cafe/Restaurant
Exhibition Hall

islands of program at ground level
site porosity

places of stay
(cross like and conditions)
rather than places of flow

programmatic relationships
ground level

programmatic relationships
upper level

unified form

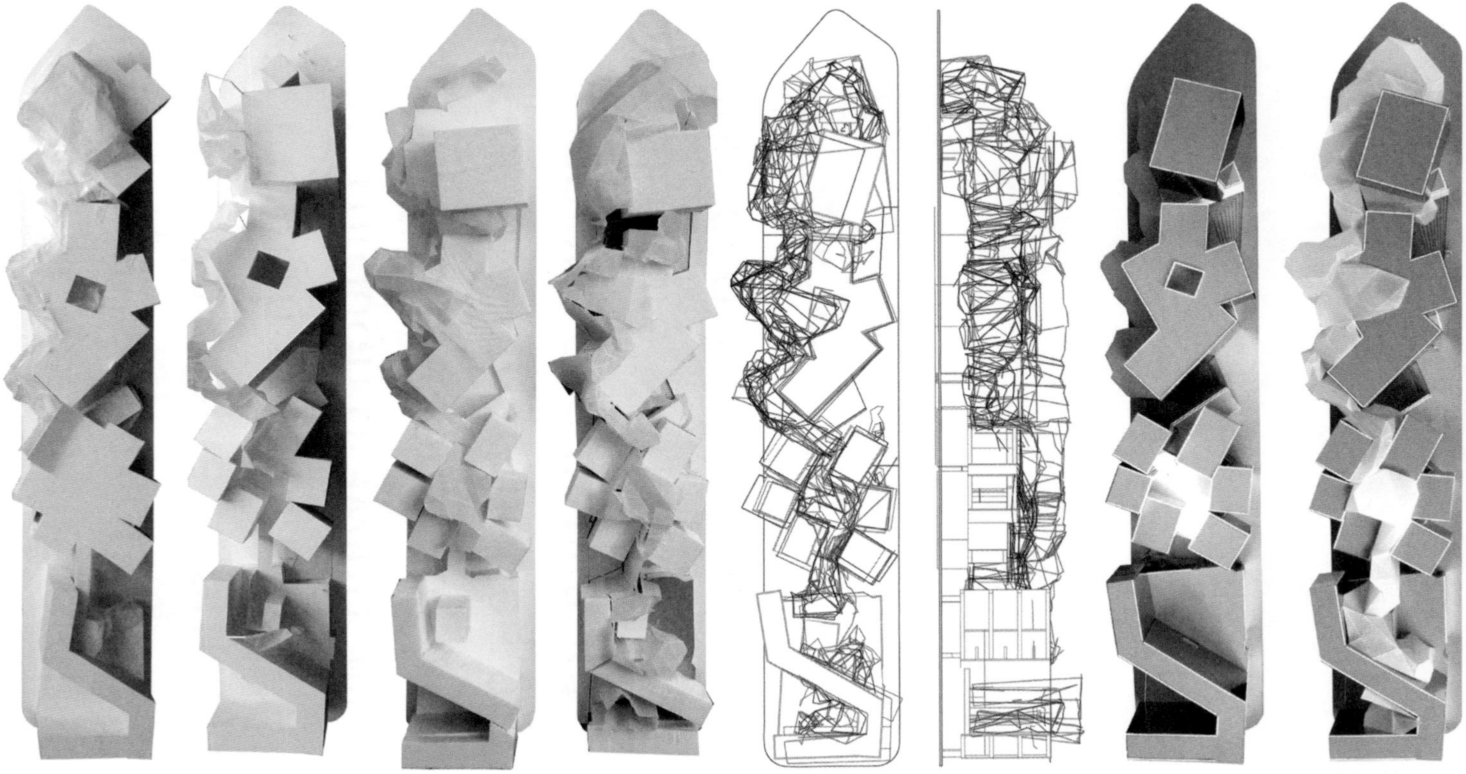

ALDA BLACK

opaque versus
transparent spaces;
art circulation space
is visible to public

art circulation space as
intervention/flexible
space

scale (heights)
and facets studies

three digitized models
plan

three digitized models
elevation

final model

Imagine New Futures

The lines of inquiry in this chapter explore the power of the architect, the landscape architect, and the urbanist to create alternative futures through speculative practice. Through drawing, film, animation, fabrication, parametric modeling, and other modes of exploration, we can construct images of future worlds, project scenarios, engage technological innovation, and establish new ways of seeing.

The Harvard University Graduate School of Design presents the first monographic exhibition on Kenzo Tange in the United States: Utopia Across Scales: Highlights from the Kenzo Tange Archive. It is the first comprehensive exhibition on Tange anywhere in the world in more than twenty years. The exhibition will draw from the Kenzo Tange Archive in Tokyo and present, for public viewing for the first time, several original models and dozens of original drawings of Tange's best-known works, including Hiroshima Peace Center, Kagawa Prefectural Government Building, and Yoyogi National Indoor Stadiums. The exhibition will also feature a visual essay on Tange's visionary plan for Tokyo Bay in 1960, reexamining the role of housing, monumentality, communication, and scale in Tange's architectural and urban thinking.

Utopia Across Scales was curated by Seng Kuan, PhD Candidate in Architecture at the Harvard University Graduate School of Design, with support from the Exhibitions Department of the GSD, and the Special Collections Department.

Distillations: Gropius_Japan_1954
In conjunction with Utopia Across Scales, the GSD's Frances Loeb Library will mount a display of remarkable photographs that Walter Gropius took during his trip to Japan in the late spring of 1954. Also showcased will be a series of key historical texts and antiquarian objects, exploring the role of the West as an interlocutor in the discourse of tradition and modernity in twentieth-century architecture in Japan. Distillations is jointly organized by Mary Daniels, head of Special Collections at the Frances Loeb Library, Seng Kuan, and Yukio Lippit, the Harris K. Weston Associate Professor of the Humanities at Harvard University.

Twenty-Five Years of the Kenzo Tange Visiting Professorship at Harvard
Also concurrent will be a retrospective display on the twenty-five-year history of the Kenzo Tange Visiting Professorship at the GSD, with an emphasis on student work produced under the guidance of the visitors. Since spring 1984, twenty-nine individuals or partnerships have been appointed to the Chair, including Alvaro Siza, Enric Miralles, Peter Zumthor, and Kazuyo Sejima. In addition, several current faculty members were also recipients of the Chair, including Rafael Moneo, Farshid Moussavi, and Jacques Herzog and Pierre de Meuron. In the fall semester of 2009, the Chair was held by Valerio Olgiati.

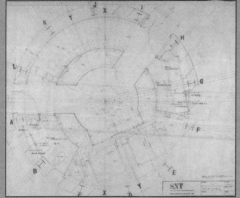

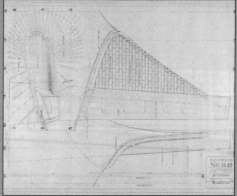

Exhibition Imagine New Futures

NEONATURES

Skyscraper collectives, agglomerations, alignments, bundles, clusters, and twins; mixed-use developments, high-rise housing developments, waterfront and marina developments, luxury condominiums; airport hubs, corporate office enclaves, industrial parks, hotel complexes, conference centers, commercial, financial centers; satellite cities, theme parks, thematic cities, new districts, gated communities: what is the potential latent in extraordinarily large urban typologies, still restricted by the typological tradition of urbanism and by the predominant segregation of disciplinary domains? What is the reach of this misused potential as a means to think aggressively about the urban environment, and as a medium to envision and breed future developmental models at a time when the relationship with nature has become one of equals?

Neo-natural architecture is the complex assemblage of extraordinarily large forms of development, and their containment, breeding, and branding through highly naturalistic artifacts, operating as single yet multiplicitous architectural compounds, at the same time volatile and sturdy. Neonatures host a variety of models of organization and degrees of urban concentration in an individual geo-architectural form, which operates as a paraphernalia of services, interior design, technology, and infrastructure. Neonatures steer unpredictable programmatic coexistences and unprecedented organizational collaborations within a poignant naturalistic being, giving substance and substantiation to an apparently prosaic take on utopia: an archaic form of power, situated beyond urban goods and evils: both 'within' nature and 'as if it were' nature.

The studio pursued the opportunity of rethinking urbanism as a blunt form of architectural grandeur, through the concept, methodology, and agenda of Neonatures. We worked on the Ecological Reserve of Buenos Aires, a site of over 300 hectares located between the city center, a large area of major development currently unfolding, and the Rio de la Plata. The Reserve was treated as a metropolitan-territorial laboratory, where new forms of 'neonatural urbanism' were experimented, configuring the means for a virtual master plan for the region. A field trip was planned to include a number of site visits, meetings with local practitioners and academicians, case studies and typological surveys in the city, and a workshop and review.

NEONATURES
TYPOLOGIES AND GEOMORPHOLOGIES

...es and Geomorphologies

Option Studio Imagine New Futures

ANA MARIA FLOR ORTIZ, RODIA VALLADARES SANCHEZ

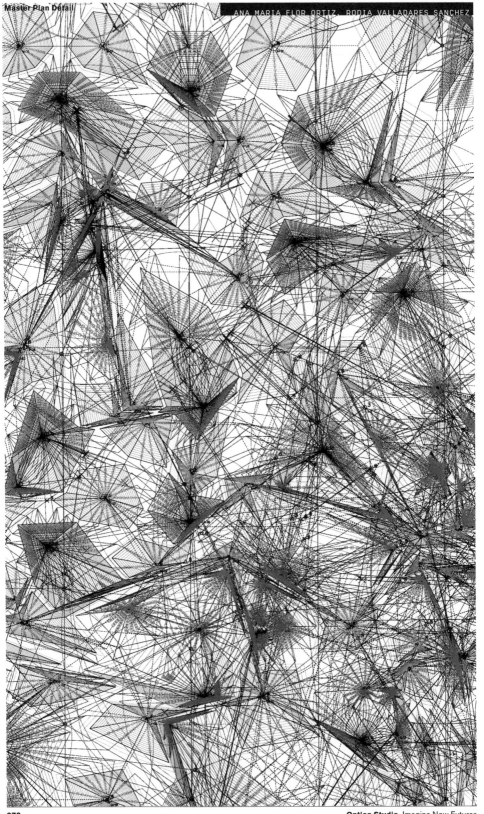

Option Studio Imagine New Futures

Shopping Rock Formation Diagram

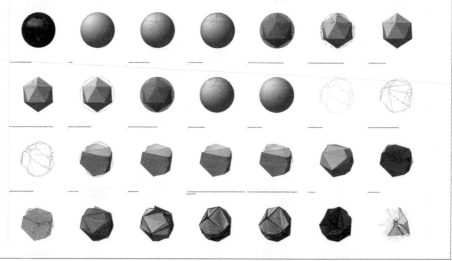

Model
KAZUAKI YONEDA

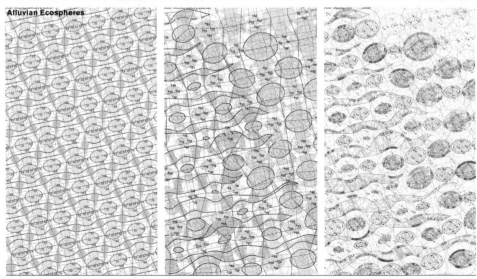

Alluvian Ecospheres

Option Studio Imagine New Futures

THE SHAPES OF UTOPIA

SEMINAR | ERIKA NAGINSKI

"You speak of that city of which we are the founders, and which exists in idea only, for I do not think there is such a one anywhere on earth..." —John Ruskin, Fors Clavigera (1874)

Utopia's fall from grace in the modern period is crucially tied to architecture's failure in giving shape to dreams of a new society wrought from social and political transformation. Its memorable articulations appear in a venerable philosophical and literary tradition, and include Plato's Republic, Augustine's City of God and Sir Thomas More's utopian city of Amaurote. Its significant disarticulations materialize in Foucault, Tafuri, and the dismal outcome of modernist projects like Pruitt-Igoe. Utopia divulges the oscillation of a concept associated alternately with arcadian pasts or ordered futures, naive idealism or repressive totalitarianism, phalansteries or simple living, mental escapism or technological promise. And the etymological variants—Eutopia, Outopia, Dystopia, Heterotopia, Extropia, Ecotopia, etc.—reveal an interdisciplinary complexity, which forces upon architectural form the intractable fabric of social realities, possibilities, and disappointments.

This seminar took a synoptic approach by considering both key writings and architectural experiments. We began with a selection of foundational texts that posited an architectural matrix for the construction of a more perfect world. We then turned to those architectural proposals, from Ledoux to Le Corbusier, that attempted to reify the guiding principles of an improved social order. We concluded with theoretical and architectural critiques emerging in modernism's wake.

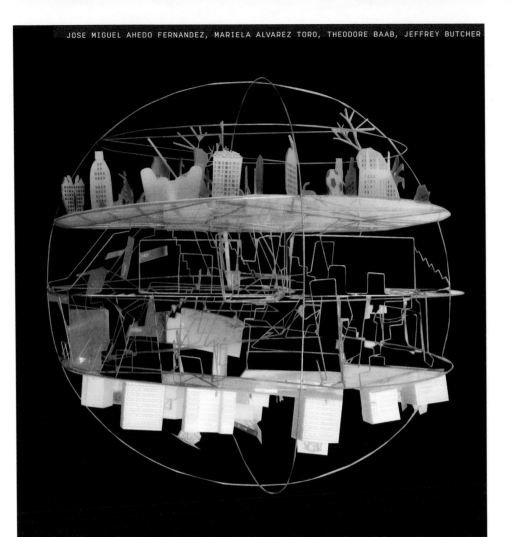

JOSE MIGUEL AHEDO FERNANDEZ, MARIELA ALVAREZ TORO, THEODORE BAAB, JEFFREY BUTCHER

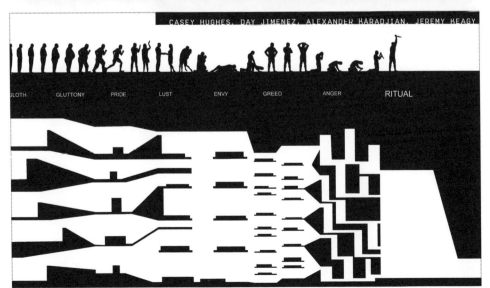

CASEY HUGHES, DAY JIMENEZ, ALEXANDER KARADJIAN, JEREMY KEAGY

SLOTH   GLUTTONY   PRIDE   LUST   ENVY   GREED   ANGER   RITUAL

PAUL DAHLKE, ROBERT DE MIGUEL, ANA MARIA FLOR ORTIZ, JEREMY GREEN

The last of a four-semester sequence of design studios concluded the introduction to architectural design by emphasizing students' elaboration and substantiation of personal ideas through complex design exercises and by critically addressing the status of contemporary architectural thought through discussion, lectures, and seminars.

The studio focused on the design of urban frameworks and the reciprocal integration of the large-scale public building within this framework. The role of nature and the environment, with all of its emerging questions of social and performance criteria, formed the underlay of the studies. Collaboration with the Landscape Architecture Core Studio GSD1212, in the form of shared lectures and team exercises, generated cross-disciplinary knowledge for both architecture and landscape students to draw from.

In the urban context, the idea of nature has merged with notions of the public sphere and all of its armatures including infrastructures, streets, and open spaces. In this way the role of public architecture becomes an inextricable extension to this relationship between nature and the city. The broader aspirations of the public building have figured prominently as a visooral and emblematic materialization of the way larger conceptions of the urban and the ecological intersect.

Within the current context of the pressing environmental crises, we must now enter into a new debate about the role of nature and the city. At this historical crossroads where nothing short of revolutionary propositions will do, we are now in the privileged position to create our own thesis about nature and the city. Through critiquing, re-reading, and synthesizing these trajectories with our own notions, we can propose more radical and necessary shifts in the urban habits and development patterns that are essentially unsustainable.

ANDREW MCGEE

Manhattan Skyline

Phasing Diagram

Through the Aquatic Center + Beyond

Building Framing Landscape, Play, Light

Recreational Isthmus Site Plan

SAMAA ELIMAM

0   500 ft   1000 ft

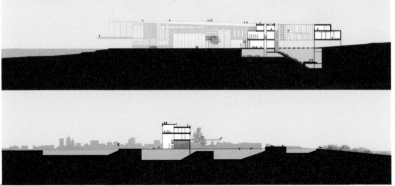

Roof-Landscape Relationship Explored through Section

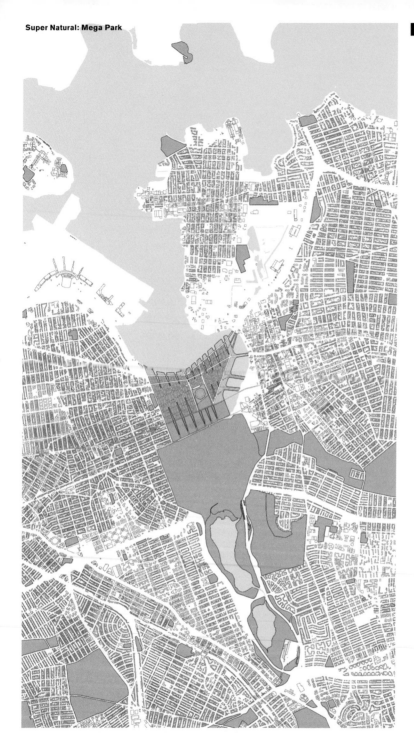

FUN CITY
Recreational & Infrastructural Green

HYUN TEK YOON

Perspective: Athletic Facility

Perspective: Atrium, Swimming Pool

ROBIN BANKERT

View from Playground

Facade Rendering from Retention Pond

PAUL MERRILL

Interior Athletic Space

Mid-Tide Aerial Rendering

This studio focused on the development of urban form as driven by ecology and environmental dynamics. It introduced students to methods and representational techniques for describing urban form and the underlying ecologies that might be invoked to shape the urban fabric. Representational strategies began with mapping and diagramming larger ecological processes and dynamics on an urban brownfield site, and then focused on the description of built form, urban infrastructure, and the relationships between the city and its reconstituted riverine setting. Early and mid-semester workshops focused on urban ecologies and parametric urbanism, respectively.

Program, Transportation, and Green Corridor

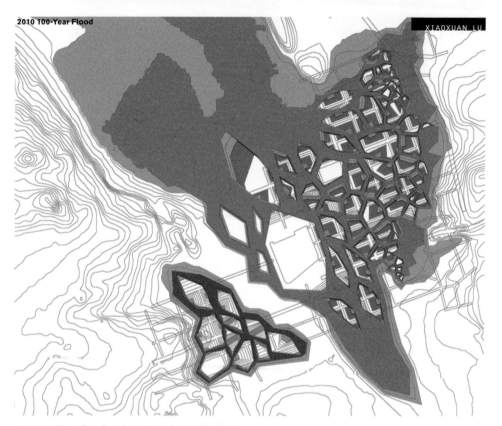

Waterway, Water Flow Speed, and Water Courtyard Network

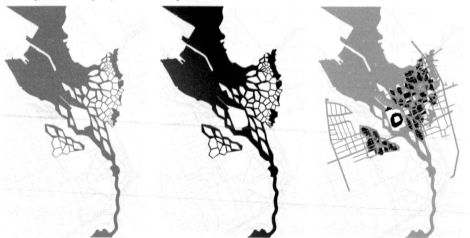

Fingers

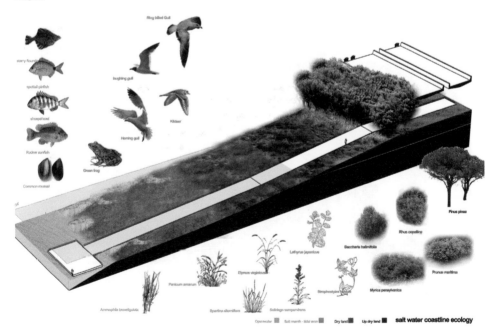

salt water coastline ecology

Open water ■ Salt marsh - tidal area ■ Dry land ■ Up dry land ■

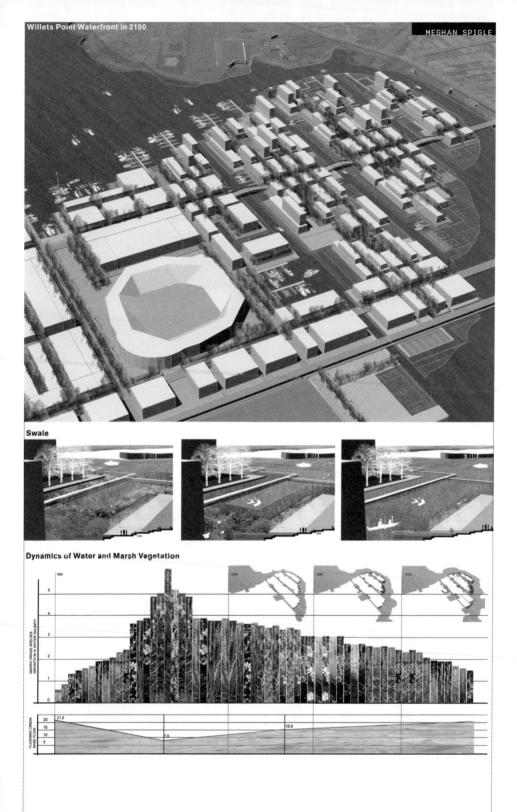

MEGHAN SPIGLE

Swale

Dynamics of Water and Marsh Vegetation

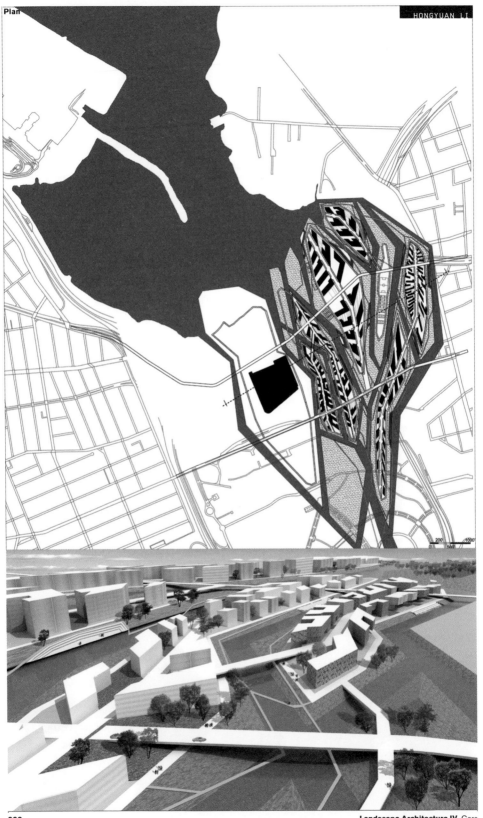

Section of Built and Canal Typology

Section of Outer Jetty Typology

Design Diagram of Fragmentation Effect and Dike Removal

DIGITAL CULTURE IN ARCHITECTURE

LECTURE ANTOINE PICON APRIL 20, 2010. EXCERPT

Tonight I would like to share a certain number of questions as hypotheses related to what is probably a major transformation of the architectural discipline, a transformation that I will not hesitate to characterize as a revolution.

One may wonder—and I do wonder sometimes—why a historian like me has devoted so much time to a phenomenon that appears extremely recent at first. I think it is, among other things, the consequence of the adoption of a broad time frame in which to examine the phenomenon. In the case of the relation between digital culture and architecture, this has led me to place the recent evolution in a much longer chronology than it had been before. I think, indeed, part of what we see today may be interpreted as a distant result of what happened with the emergence of an information-based society at the turn of the ninetoenth century.

As you can see here, the offices of the Prudential company at the turn of the nineteenth and twentieth century; this is the moment when information—data—becomes a crucial dimension of social and corporate life. Another series of changes appear as a consequence of the rise of the computer, both as a machine and as a vision of the world at the end of the Second World War. Later episodes like the development of the Internet played, of course, a decisive role in today's development.

At the various stages of this extended chronology, one finds a series of interactions between information, computing, and communication on the one hand and architecture, urban planning, and urban design on the other.

To be truly revolutionary, a transformation must appear both as
extremely recent and dramatic, and
as something that corresponds to a
much longer and progressive evolution. Otherwise, it would be a mere
incident.

Despite its crucial role, the computer is only one aspect of
a transformation that is fundamentally social and cultural.
It's not the computer that has created the society of
information, since the advent of this society predates the
computer by something like fifty to sixty years. As I said, it
begins, really, in the last decades of the nineteenth century.
Similarly, it seems to me that the development of digital
architecture is not reducible to the mere use of a new
tool. It is inseparable from a much broader cultural frame.
Actually, architecture has not been passively subjected to
a technological innovation coming from elsewhere. In other
words, I think in the affair, there is an agency of architecture
that must not be underestimated. It's more two things
that meet than the computer invading architecture, as it's
sometimes presented.

Traditionally—and this is true of other domains than design, by the way—information-gathering graphic production was a tedious process in which the technicalities of design were often of a doubting nature, and it's true that now, the computer enables designers to navigate more fluid sets of data, parameters, and geometric and technological solutions. So this fluidity, gives a crucial importance to the question of the strategy used to navigate successfully this informational environment. In other words, the question of the "Why?" has become, often, more import than the "How?" And this is probably, for me, the main paradox today: The coexistence of an extremely strong tendency towards formalism on the one hand, and on the other hand, of all sorts of attempts to go beyond that.

Now, we have had a new impetus in this question of how to go beyond form, thanks to all the perspectives opened by parametric design, scripting, algorithmic, etc.—a path explored at all kinds of levels. Behind that, we have a serious question, which is, "Should we still concentrate on the definition of an architectural object, or rather, try to construct parameters, relations, and a series of operations enabling its production?" Indeed, what we can do today with a computer is, in some ways, design abstract machines' set of relation and instructions that can produce families of possible objects. I think the real question today is, "At what level are we going to design in the future? What will design mean?" The nature and scale of design operations might very well be on the eve of a transformation comparable in its scope to what happened at the time of the invention of perspective at the Renaissance.

What I would argue is that now, instead of being thought of as a thing, form becomes commensurable with an event. Form happens. It is essentially active and it can be a critical part of the various scenarios that we mobilize to think about the future.

What is at stake is the desire for a new and more intimate connection between the architectural object and its environment—an environment that is not reducible to the old notion of context—that represents something of a more dynamic nature. The traditional status of architecture as plenitude and presence is radically challenged by this evolution.

MEDIUMS

The hypothesis of the studio was that the problems of medium specificity can be addressed by exacerbating multiple medium specificities into impure, awkward, and paradoxical recombinations. The goal was to be as specific and detailed as possible while assembling a series of competing mediums into a project.

As an open laboratory in search of alternative architectural models, these investigations were anchored by several texts concerning mediums and the post-medium condition.

Studio participants developed a highly self-conscious diagramming and working mini-history of at least one medium of their choosing, and an understanding of the modalities of medium itself. Site and program, the usual ingredients of a studio project, were just two of many possible mediums to be considered and understood. Both are characteristics of different perhaps competing architectural regimes. Our site was The High Line in Manhattan, and the program was a Unitarian church. Additionally, we investigated interactive processes, animation, and film as methods of architectural representation. These mediums, among others, were operating in parallel with each other and at times directly competing with each other. The hierarchies of multiple mediums can be determined either through an absolute hierarchy or a relative one. (For instance, the problems of concrete material construction could trump a perfectly precise algorithmic geometry, etc.) These relationships were described and mapped out. Through a careful teasing out of mediums, both obvious and latent, students attempted to develop an architecture for a post-medium condition, to generate what Rosalind Krauss calls differential specificity through the committed interrogation and recombination of mediums.

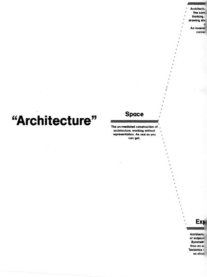

"Architecture"

Space

An Abbreviated Narrative of Medium Specificity in Architecture

The conception of medium is based upon the equation: *Medium (technical support) + Convention (artistic genre, typology, history) + Play (improvisation, !@#?) = Architecture*
In this formula medium is conceptualized as the method in which design is manifested. It is the base condition from which the act of design begins.

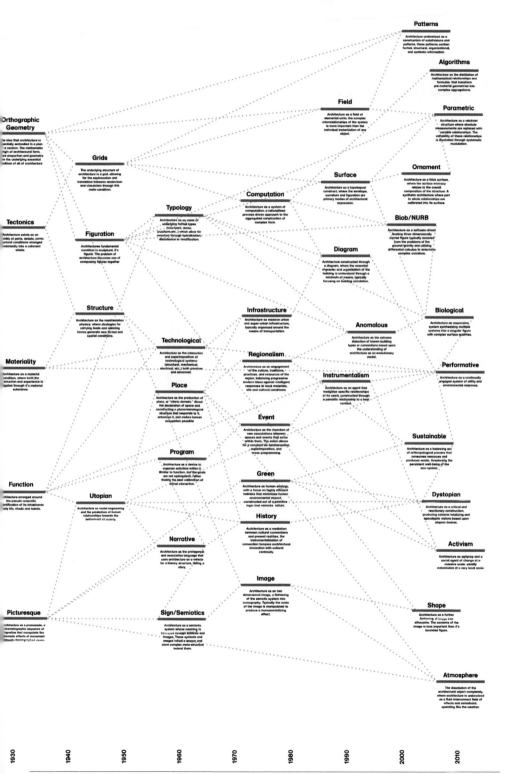

Patterns
Architecture understood as a construction of subdivisions and patterns. these patterns contain formal, structural, organizational, and symbolic information.

Algorithms
Architecture as the distillation of mathematical relationships and formulas. that transform pre-material geometries into complex aggregations.

Orthographic Geometry
the idea that architecture is essentially embodied in a plan or a section. The mathematical origin of architectural form, are proportion and geometry are the underlying essential condition of all of architecture

Grids
The underlying structure of architecture is a grid, allowing for the equivocation and translation between modernism and classicism through this meta-condition.

Field
Architecture as a field of elemental units, the complex interrelationships of the system is more important than the individual instantiation of any object.

Parametric
Architecture as a relativist structure where absolute measurements are replaced with variable relationships. The variability of these relationships are illustrated through systematic modulation.

Surface
Architecture as a topological construct, where the envelope, curvature and figuration are primary modes of architectural expression.

Ornament
Architecture as a thick surface, where the surface relates to the overall composition of the structure. A synthetic architecture where part to whole relationships are calibrated into its surface.

Computation
Architecture as a system of computation, a rationalized process driven approach to the aggregated construction of complex form.

Typology
Architecture as an index of underlying formal types (box/yard, dome, cruciform.etc..) which allow for mutation through hybridization, disturbance or modification.

Tectonics
Architecture exists as an entity of parts, details, joints. structural conditions arranged consistently into a coherent whole.

Figuration
Architectures fundamental condition is sculptural, it's figural. The problem of architecture becomes one of composing figures together

Blob/NURB
Architecture as a software-driven floating three dimensionally curved figure typically removed from the problems of the ground/gravity and utilizing differential calculus to determine complex curvature.

Diagram
Architecture constructed through a diagram, where the essential character and organization of the building is understood through a minimum of means, typically focusing on building circulation.

Structure
Architecture as the manifestation physics, where strategies for carrying loads and resisting forces generate new formal and spatial conditions.

Infrastructure
Architecture as massive urban and super-urban infrastructure, typically organized around the means of transportation.

Anomalous
Architecture as the extreme distortion of known building types or conventions based upon the understanding of architecture as an evolutionary model.

Biological
Architecture as responsive, system synthesizing multiple systems into a singular figure with complex surface qualities.

Materiality
Architecture as a material condition, where both the sensation and experience is ignited through it's material substance.

Technological
Architecture as the intersection and superimposition of technological systems (structural, mechanical, electrical, etc..) both primitive and advanced.

Regionalism
Architecture as an engagement of the culture, traditions, practices, and resources of the region, balancing progressive modern ideas against intelligent responses to local materials, site and cultural conditions.

Instrumentalism
Architecture as an agent that instigates specific relationships of its users, constructed through a parasitic relationship to a host context.

Performative
Architecture as a continually engaged system of utility and environmental response.

Place
Architecture as the production of place, or "etherial domain." About the declaration of space and constructing a phenomenological structure that responds to it, enhances it, and makes human occupation possible

Event
Architecture as the invention of new associations between spaces and events that occur within them. The event allows for a constant de-familiarization, superimposition, and cross-programming.

Sustainable
Architecture as a balancing act of anthropological process that consumes resources and produces waste, threatening the persistent well-being of the eco-system.

Function
architecture arranged around the pseudo-scientific justification of its inhabitants daily life, rituals and habits.

Program
Architecture as a device to organize activities within it. Similar to function, but the goals are not optimization, rather finding the best calibration of social interaction.

Green
Architecture as human etiology, with a focus on highly efficient habitats that minimizes human environmental impact, constructed out of a primitive logic that mimicks nature.

Utopian
Architecture as social engineering and the production of human relationships towards the betterment of society.

Dystopian
Architecture as a critical and reactionary construction, producing extreme totalizing and apocalyptic visions based upon utopian desires.

History
Architecture as a mediation between cultural conventions and present realities, the instrumentalization of convention tempers architectural innovation with cultural continuity.

Narrative
Architecture as the protagonist and associative language that uses architecture as a vehicle for a literary structure, telling a story.

Activism
Architecture as agitprop and a social agent of change at a massive scale, usually instantiated at a very local scale.

Image
Architecture as two dimensional image, a flattening of the semotic system into iconography. Typically the scale of the image is manipulated to produce a monumentalizing effect.

Picturesque
architecture as a promenade, a cinematographic sequence of vignettes that manipulate the kinematic effects of movement through choreographed views.

Sign/Semiotics
Architecture as a semiotic system whose meaning is conveyed through symbols and images. These symbols and images reveal a deeper and more complex meta-structure beyond them.

Shape
Architecture as a further flattening of image into silhouette. The contents of the image is less important than it's bounded figure.

Atmosphere
The dissolution of the architectural object completely, where architecture is understood as a fluid interconnect field of effects and sensations. operating like the weather.

| 1930 | 1940 | 1950 | 1960 | 1970 | 1980 | 1990 | 2000 | 2010 |

ANDREW DOMNITZ

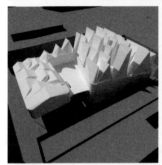

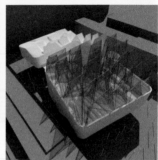

Grainy Orbit

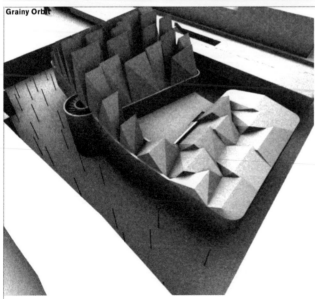

MATT STORUS

ON THE BRI(N)CK:
ARCHITECTURE OF THE ENVELOPE

SEMINAR INGEBORG ROCKER

The seminar-workshop traced the historical development of a debate concerning the architectural envelope beginning at the end of the nineteenth century. It was then when new materials and technologies became available and began to inform architecture and discussions led in its behalf. Architects began to question the role mass-production should play in architecture, as much as they questioned the influence of new notation and construction techniques on the architects' work. Today these and similar questions gain a new relevance as the digital medium literally informs the conceptualization and production of architecture.

A directed reading sequence of primary texts encircled a spectrum of possible answers. Assigned group presentations focused on the critical analysis of case studies through drawing and writing. Hands-on workshops on digital fabrication supplemented the analytic inquiry with the aim to produce speculative envelope-models using the school's CAD/CAM facilities.

Emphasizing equally reading, writing, graphic analysis, and numerically controlled fabrication, the seminar-workshop suggested a method of research that bridges between architecture's practices.

Topics included: technical and discursive development of architectural envelopes; mass-production/mass-customization; mechanization/digitization; abstraction/expressionism.

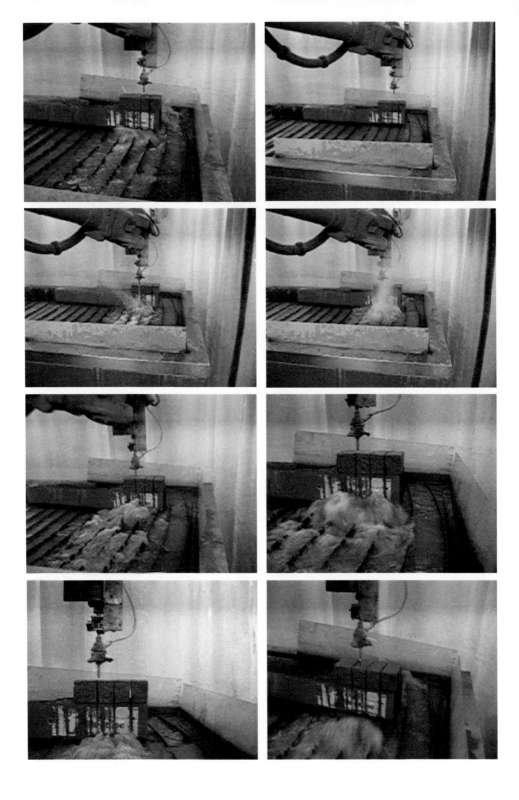

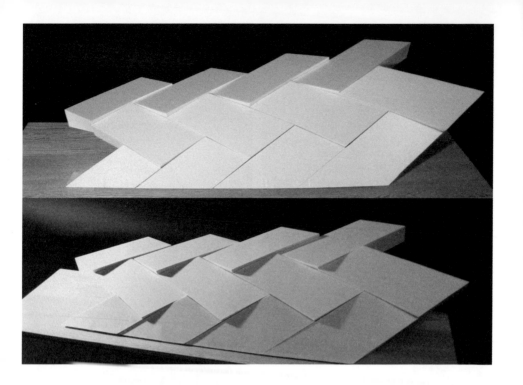

Creating a museum without artifacts is an opportunity for researching new design strategies for immersive projection environments. In "TRACES" we investigated the relationship between projected content, physical form, materials, and space. This timely topic has been previously explored on the scale of installations, but remains poorly understood when expanded to an entire museum. The studio was based on the premise that design strategies must simultaneously consider (and design) both the projected content and the physical nature of the spatial environment. The physical and virtual prototyping of projection environments was an integral part of the studio's experimentation. Fabrication studies investigated the interplay between material surfaces and projections of still and moving images.

"TRACES" challenged students to implement their design strategies in proposals for a museum environment dedicated to the Armenian Genocide in Yerevan, the capital of Armenia. The mass killing of Armenian's by Ottoman Turks towards the end of the Ottoman Empire has since been a highly sensitive political subject. The possibility of realizing a new museum is currently being discussed in Armenia—hence providing a realistic context for the studio. Students collaborated with the existing Genocide Museum and Institute in Yerevan, and explored an intervention that merges architecture and landscape in the area of Dzidzernakapert. A field trip to Armenia to allow for in-depth on-site research and exploration was planned.

While the specificity of the program was crucial, the studio was interested in replicable design strategies for dealing with the emerging typology of immersive and responsive environments. The studio was funded by Armenia's Luys Foundation with the participation of Tufenkian Heritage Hotels.

Sunken Corridor

Morning View of Semi-Artificial Projection Space

MOJTABA ANSARI, JAE MIN HA

Paying Tribute

Transformation of Text with Change in the Direction of Light

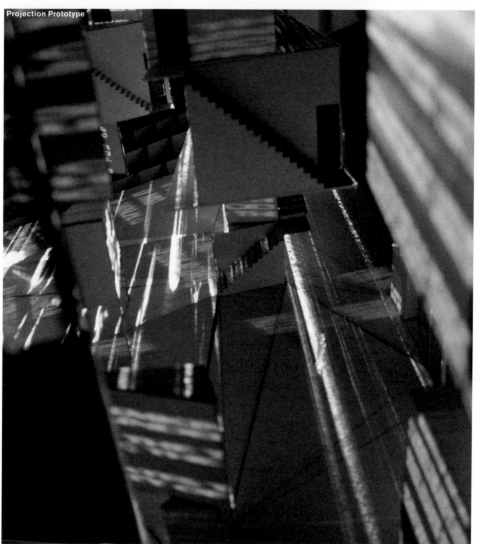

Sections

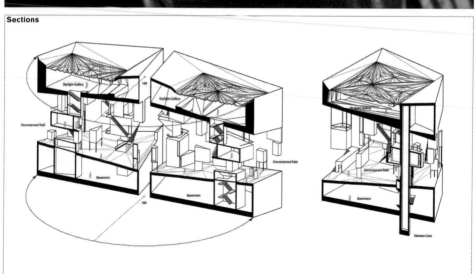

Projection Decomposition

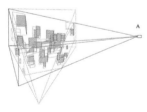

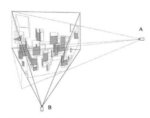

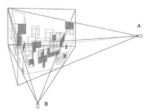

Surfaces for projector A   Surfaces for projector B   Surfaces for both projectors

"IT'S BEAUTIFUL...BUT WHO NEEDS AN ENDLESS BENCH?": AGONY, HYPOCRISY, AND ROBOTS

M ARCH THESIS | BRETT ALBERT

ADVISOR: PRESTON SCOTT COHEN

Throughout history, architecture has engaged in a cyclical tradition of dissecting, perverting or reappropriating its own conventions to produce strange or disturbing effects during periods of great social change or uncertainty, with the intention of explicating emergent cultural antagonisms and disrupting complacent discourses.

Contemporary architecture has either failed to or opted not to engage this necessary practice, even though there have been major recent changes to our world, due primarily to the rise of digital culture and the proliferation of networks.

This thesis is composed of four scenarios that attempt to critically engage users with their environments by provoking and demanding psychic reconciliation of contradictory formal, linguistic, and sensory structures, each one couched within a particular contemporary trope with its own set of conventions and expectations that are ultimately redeployed or manipulated in startling ways: performative ornament, parametric urbanism, social justice, and sustainability.

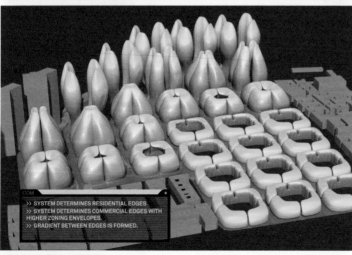

COM
>> SYSTEM DETERMINES RESIDENTIAL EDGES
>> SYSTEM DETERMINES COMMERCIAL EDGES WITH
HIGHER ZONING ENVELOPES.
>> GRADIENT BETWEEN EDGES IS FORMED.

FIVE VIEWPOINTS ON DIGITALLY AUGMENTED SPACES

DDES THESIS NASHID NABIAN

ADVISOR: ANTOINE PICON

Nashid Nabian's dissertation offers one of the most comprehensive analyses of digitally augmented reality. Dealing with questions such as the interplay between the contemporary definition of the individual and digital augmentation or the role of networks in the evolution of spatial representations and practices, her work combines deftly theoretical considerations and experimental realizations.

—Antoine Picon

The dissertation explores design practices of non-intrusively augmenting inhabitable spaces with digital and telecommunication technologies. The theoretical part critically evaluates approaches to designing augmented environments from five different, yet closely connected networks of thoughts and speculations: spatiality, temporality, subjectivity, technology, and the network condition. The practical part involves three case studies that explore the possibility of designing material-digital hybrid spaces that are inhabited and occupied by contemporary subjects, as established in the theoretical framework; rely heavily on the technological constructs of monitoring, actuation, computing, geo-localization, and networking; and are closely connected to the idea of the temporalization of space and real-time access to information. A brief description of each project is as follows:

MIT GEOBlog is a platform for digitally annotating space for the purpose of collective, community-based, digital story telling. GEOBlog's web-based platform allows people to annotate its virtual space through geo-tagging and sharing user-generated content, or in other words, placing digital content over spatial zones, so that this content can be retrieved by others based on the system sensing and locating them in real-time and in physical space.

Lochaber Live with Mounted Mobile Camera Casts is a platform that allows a real-time feed of multiple cameras mounted on mobile human or non-human entities to be delivered wirelessly, via a 3G and beyond network. The multiple, mobile, real-time casts will be available on a Web interface or a broadcasted channel where the real-time location/orientation of each mobile agent is also visible on a navigable interactive map, along with other contextual information that allows users to be able to locate the point of view they're seeing in real-time, conveniently conveying the sensations attached to experiencing a landscape.

Lochaber Live with Smart Signs focuses on the enhancement of tourist-oriented information delivery systems by augmenting conventional commercial signs with digital technology in order to deliver real-time information both in-situ and via distance. The new, technologically augmented signs allow the user to report the real-time availability of a specific service to the Web-based application. The aggregate data gathered from all the smart signs would be visualized on a map via the Web.

What if instead of one Big Brother filming everybody, we allow everybody to become a Little Sister...a concept illustration inspired by Steve Mann's elaboration on surveillance.

BOSTON BOTANY BAY:
THE NAKED GARDEN AS SPECTACLE
OF PLANT PSYCHO-GEOGRAPHY

OPTION STUDIO | BRIDGET BAINES, EELCO HOOFTMAN

The Boston Botany Bay studio attempted to redefine the concept of the botanical garden for the 21st century. The archipelago of islands in the Boston Harbor became a testing ground for new and stimulating ideas of how to celebrate, utilize and research the wonders of plants. Nature activation, instead of nature conservation, was the focus of the studio. Nature is to be considered the raw material—both a resource and a product of new bioengineered technologies, endless modifications and stimulating hybridizations between organic and inorganic matter. How can the botanic garden of the 21st century contribute towards new economical, environmental, aesthetic and scientific demand? Can the botanic garden, the metropolis of plants, become a pretext for future urbanization?

The aim of the studio was to generate, test, and document contemporary notions of the botanic garden of the future. We focused on three complementary activities—research, strategy, and design. Studio research was edited and presented in magazine format based upon the format of "Garden and Forest," the illustrious magazine of the 1880's. The strategy focused upon a long-term botanic vision for the entire Boston Bay, which is regarded as an integrated coastal zone; a unique morphology based upon a combination of natural phenomena and the interaction of man. As part of the strategy a series of prototypes were developed and tested as representative of the overall approach. These prototype projects should operate as "agent provocateur" to initiate change. Finally, for the design stage each student addressed one selected island and produced detailed resolutions representing the botanic garden of the 21st century.

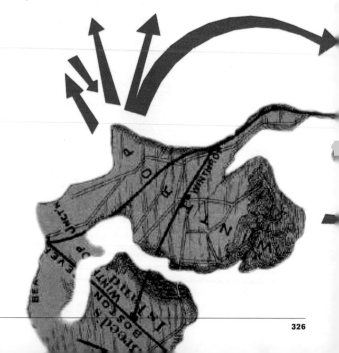

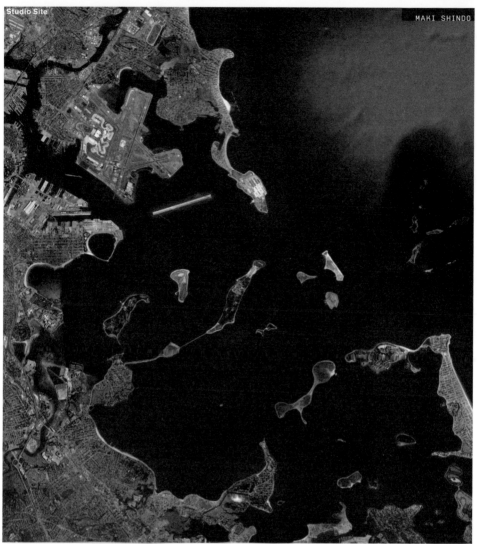
Studio Site

MAKI SHINDO

Viewing Platform + Soil Storage Dyke

Imagine New Futures **Option Studio**

Great Brewster Island Plan, Elevation, Analysis

MI YANG

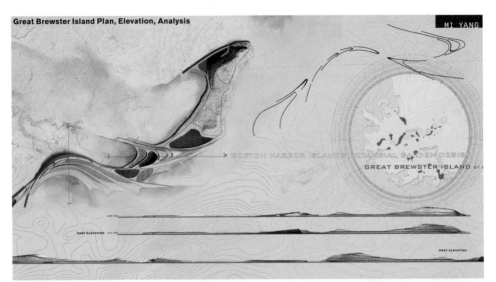

Great Brewster Island Perspective

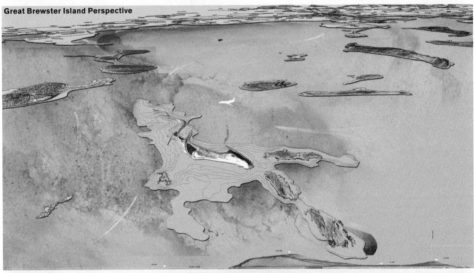

Wave Viewer

ANDREW ZIENTEK

Option Studio Imagine New Futures

Site Plan

Perspective

Imagine New Futures **Option Studio**

330

Option Studio Imagine New Futures

VIVIEN LIU

APPENDIX

GSD FACULTY PUBLICATIONS

LECTURE SERIES AND EVENTS

STUDENT GROUP ACTIVITIES

STAFF

GSD Platform 2
Felipe Correa, editor
Actar/GSD

A View on Harvard GSD Vol 2
Tank/GSD

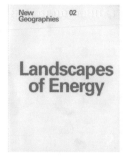

New Geographies 02
Landscapes of Energy
Rania Ghosn, Editor-in-chief
GSD

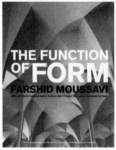

The Function of Form
Farshid Moussavi, author
Daniel Lopez, Garrick Ambrose,
Ben Fortunato, Ryan Ludwig, and
Ahmadreza Schricker, editors
Actar/GSD

Interactive Architecture Design
Dr. Carlos Calderon
GSD

Invention/Transformation:
Strategies for the Qattara/Jimi
Oases in Al Ain
Felipe Correa and Jorge Silvetti,
editors
GSD

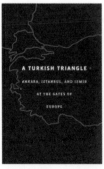

A Turkish Triangle: Ankara,
Istanbul, and Izmir at the Gates
of Europe
Aga Khan Program Book Series
Hashim Sarkis, editor
GSD

The Architecture and Memory of
the Minority Quarter in the Muslim
Mediterranean City
Aga Khan Program Book Series
Susan Gilson Miller and Mauro Bertagnin,
editors
GSD

On Asphalt
Paula Meijerink
GSD

Alejandro de la Sota
Iñaki Ábalos, Josep Llinàs and
Moisés Puente, editors
Fundación Caja de Arquitectos

**Naturaleza y artificio
part of Compendios de
Arquitectura series**
Iñaki Ábalos
GG - Gustavo Gili

**Michael Van Valkenburgh
Associates: Reconstructing
Urban Landscapes**
Anita Berrizbeitia, editor
Yale University Press

**Olafur Eliasson: Your Chance
Encounter**
Olafur Eliasson Studio, editors
Eve Blau, contributor
Lars Müller

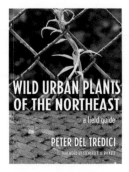

**Wild Urban Plants of the
Northeast: A Field Guide**
Peter Del Tredici
Cornell University Press/
Comstock Book

Ecological Urbanism
Mohsen Mostafavi and Gareth
Doherty, editors
Lars Müller

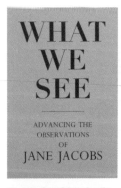

**What We See: Advancing the
Observations of Jane Jacobs**
Lynne Elizabeth and Stephen
Goldsmith, editors
James Stockard, contributor
New Village Press

**Architecture's Desire:
Reading the Late Avante-
Garde**
K. Michael Hays
MIT Press

**Expanded Practice: Höweler
+ Yoon Architecture/MY
Studio** Eric Höweler
Princeton Architectural Press

Mrs. Delany and Her Circle
Mark Laird, editor
Yale University Press

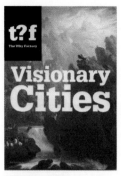

Visionary Cities
Winy Maas, Alexander
Sverdlov, Emily Waugh, editors
NAi Publishers

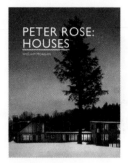

Peter Rose: Houses
William Morgan
Princeton Architectural Press

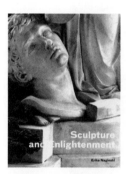

Sculpture and Enlightenment
Erika Naginski
Getty Publications

**Digital Culture in
Architecture: An Introduction
for the Design Professions**
Antoine Picon, editor
Birkhauser Verlag

HARVARD DESIGN MAGAZINE

Harvard University
Graduate School of Design
Architecture
Landscape architecture
Urban planning and design
Fall/Winter 2009/10

31

$23 US/28.95 CDN

(Sustainability)
+ Pleasure, vol. II:
Landscapes,
Urbanism,
and Products

**Harvard Design Magazine
Number 31 (Sustainability) +
Pleasure, vol. II: Landscapes,
Urbanism, and Products**
William S. Saunders, editor
Fall/Winter 2009–10
GSD

Harvard Design Magazine
Number 32
Design Practices Now, vol. I
William S. Saunders, editor
Spring/Summer 2010
GSD

ISN'T THERE A RISING OUT OF THE EARTH OF GREATER AND GREATER PRESSURES TO THINK ABOUT LARGE SCALE ECOLOGIES? DO ECOLOGICAL PRESSURES CHANGE ARCHITECTURE IN SOME KEY WAY?

David Adjaye
Adjaye Associates

David Adjaye, Nobel Peace Center/Nobel Fredssenter, Oslo, 2005. Courtesy David Adjaye

International Practices

Mohsen Mostafavi

WHY ECOLOGICAL URBANISM?
WHY NOW?

Preamble—The world's population continues to grow, resulting in a steady migration from rural to urban areas. Increased numbers of people and cities go hand in hand with a greater exploitation of the world's limited resources. Every year, more cities are feeling the devastating impacts of this situation. What means do we have as designers to address this challenging reality?

Dallas Clayton, The New York City Waterfalls/Brooklyn Bridge, 2008. Commissioned by Public Art Fund. © Dallas Clayton, 2008. Waterfalls, Olafur Eliasson. Photographs courtesy of Public Art Fund.

Conclusions

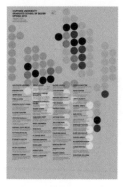

Fall Lecture Series

Spring Lecture Series

Technology Lecture Series
10.15.09 // Augmented Reality in Art & Design
11.12.09 // Adaptive & Self-Reflective Systems
11.19.09 // Material Progeny
03.29.10 // Adaptive Environments

Now? Lecture Series
09.10.09 // Public Projections
& Instrumentations
10.19.09 // Curating - 3 Models
10.29.09 // Ideas on the Art, Science
& Design of Taste
2.23.10 // Now or Never?
3.24.10 // Works & Humanitarian Activities

**Max Bond, Multiculturalism,
and Social Equity in the Built
Environment**

**Convergent Flux: Extended
Topographies and the Korean
Urban Condition**

**RISK and the CITY: The Case
of Istanbul**

**Materiality & Construction:
Five Positions in
Contemporary Swiss
Architecture**

**Design Firm Leadership
Conference**

Critical Ecologies // On the
Biological, Horticultural and
Anthropological Antecedents to
Design

Cambridge Talks IV //
Design Politics

The Mathematics of Sensible
Things

Traces // Projections on Armenia:
Designing a New Genocide Museum

Inside/Out // Exploring
Gender and Space in Life,
Culture, and Art

The Return of Nature
09.16.09 // Organicism Contra Ornament
11.17.09 // The Sublime Plan
02.24.10 // The Apparatus of Sustainability
03.31.10 // The Nature of Information
04.13.10 // The Nature of Architecture

The Future of Landscape History
02.04.10 // Geographies of Modernity
02.18.10 // Representations of Modernity
03.04.10 // Instruments of Modernity
04.08.10 // On the Future of Landscape
History

LECTURES

Manuel Bailo + Rosa Rull
European Design Circle
+ Latin GSD
10.30.2009

Aziza Chaouni //
Landscape Lunchbox:
Developing Infra-Tectures
Club MEDINA
11.01.2009

Dr. John Todd
Green Design
11.06.2009

Tamaho Shigemura, Osamu
Murao, Takashi Iba, Shohei
Matsukawa // Mecha Kucha
Japan GSD
11.09.2009

Paisajes Emergentes //
Projects, Competitions +
Methods
Latin GSD
11.12.2009

Thomas Shipley //
Unitization of Space and Time
Urban Mobilities
11.19.2009

Woo Kyung Sim //
Protection of Cultural
Diversity from the Landscape
Point of View
Korea GSD
11.20.2009

Yoon Gyoo Jang //
City_Compound
Korea GSD
02.08.2010

Seung Hoy Kim //
Speed and Architecture
Korea GSD
02.17.2010

Takaharu + Yui Tezuka //
Recent Works + Challenges
Japan GSD
02.18.2010

Convergent Flux: Extended
Topographies and the Korean
Urban Condition Roundtable
Korea GSD
02.22.2010

Christian Freksa // COGNI.
TECTURES. Spatial
Structures: Design for Spatial
Computing
Urban Mobilities
03.04.2010

Starting Your Own
Development Firm
Harvard GSD Real Estate Club
+ Harvard Student Real Estate
Consortium
03.24.2010

Moshe Bar // COGNI.
TECTURES. Aesthetics:
Visual Opinions in Mind and
Brain
Urban Mobilities
03.25.2010

Dr. Farha Ghannam //
Mobile Women, Immobile
Men? Class, Gender and
Embodiment in Urban Egypt
Club MEDINA
04.01.2010

Lyndon Neri + Rossana Hu //
Breaking Boundaries:
Designing in Asia II
Asia GSD
04.07.2010

Alejandro Aravena //
Architectural Agency: The
Case of Elemental
Latin GSD
04.12.2010

Raed Jarrar // Politics +
Post War Reconstruction:
A First Hand Experience of
Occupation
SoCA
04.16.2010

Mark Igou & Scott Duncan
A Country in Transition:
Building Contemporary India
India GSD
04.26.2010

EXHIBITIONS

History of Korea
Korea GSD
02.07–02.13.2010

2009 Gwangju Design
Biennale Exhibition
Korea GSD
02.21–02.27.2010

Student Exhibition //
Affordable Housing
Development Competition
Housing GSD
04.01 - 04.30.2010

FILM SCREENINGS

Caramel
Club MEDINA
10.23.2009

Pulcinella
Ballet GSD
11.05.2009

Ballet Mécanique
Ballet GSD
11.05.2009

Koyaanisqatsi
Green Design
11.06.2009

Door to the Sky
Club MEDINA
11.13.2009

Dark Days
Housing GSD
11.19.2009

Manufactured Landscapes
Land GSD
11.20.2009

Tokyo Story
Japan GSD
02.11.2010

Olympic Games
Tourism Club
02.12–02.28.2010

Waltz with Bashir
Club MEDINA
02.26.2010

The Twin Cities
Shenzhen/Hong Kong: City of
Expiration and Regeneration
China GSD
02.26.2010

Subprimed
Housing GSD
03.29.2010

Division Street
Green Design
04.02.2010

Student Groups 2009–10 Architecture for Humanity Boston GSD // Asia GSD // BalletGSD // Beer n Dogs // Build Club // Canada GSD // China GSD // Christian Community // Club MEDINA // Critical Digital // Design with Animals // Harvard European Design Circle // Green Design // Harvard MIT Design Computation Club // Harvard Urban Planning Organization (HUPO) // Housing GSD // India GSD //

Fierce Pussy Artist Collective
Out Design + Women in Design
10.13.2009

**Rob Gogan // Towards Zero
Campus Waste: How Harvard
can be a Zero Waste/Full
Value Campus**
Green Design + GSD Green
Team
10.14.2009

**TBADDED // Student
Lecture Series Roundtable
Discussion: Architecture for
the Underserved**
Student Forum
02.12.2010

**Andy Smith and David Fox //
Architects as Stooges for the
Business of Greed**
SoCA
02.25.2010

**Jesse Louis-Rosenberg //
BRAIN.STORMS: Nervous
System Presentation**
Critical Digital
03.01.2010

Holley Chan
Green Design
03.04.2010

**Age and the Future: A Case in
Cusco, Peru**
Latin GSD
03.25.2010

**Julie Campoli // How Dense
Can You Get?**
Green Design
03.29.1010

Ciro Najle // BRAIN.STORMS
Critical Digital
03.31.2010

**Bjarke Ingels // Breaking
Boundaries: Designing in
Asia**
Asia GSD
04.02.2010

**Toma Plejic + Lea Pelivan //
Studio Up**
Harvard European Design Circle
04.05.2010

Goodiepal // BRAIN.STORMS
Critical Digital
04.08.2010

**SZHKB: Shenzhen + Hong
Kong Bi-City Biennale of
Urbanism/Architecture:**
China GSD
04.12.2010

**TBADDED // Japantowns and
Little Saigons: Immigration
and the Landscapes of
Cultural Heritage**
HUPO
04.13.2010

**Kristina Johnson // Building
a Green Energy Economy
through Accelerated
Innovation**
GSD Green Team
04.13.2010

**Beth Tauke // Inclusive
Design in the 21st Century:
More than Accessibility**
SoCA
04.19.2010

Ben Fry // BRAIN.STORMS
Critical Digital
04.20.2010

**Arab Hip Hop Artisits //
Cross-Cultural Critics**
Club MEDINA
+ Harvard Center for Middle
Eastern Studies Outreach Center
05.01.2010

Giselle
BalletGSD
10.06.2009

World Passions
BalletGSD
10.29.2009

Halloween Bash
Student Forum
10.30.2009

Beaux Arts Ball: Part Animal
Student Forum
03.27.2010

School BBQ
Student Forum
09.01.2010
05.06.2010

Staff + Faculty Awards
Student Forum
09.01.2010
05.06.2010

Student Group Fair
Student Forum
09.11.2010

**Conference // German
Conference at Harvard/
Addressing Global
Challenges: Directions for a
New Decade**
Harvard European Design Circle
02.19.2010

**Tour // Boston HOPE VI
Public Housing Tour**
Housing GSD
04.14.2010

**Publication // 2nd Annual
Student Zine - Outside/In**
Women in Design
+ Trays + Project on Spatial
Sciences
04.15–04.16.2010

**Symposium // Aligning
Interests: Delivering
Affordable and Mixed-Income
Housing**
Housing GSD
04.20.2010

**Publication // Beyond no. 1 –
Scenarios and Speculations
Bookazine Launch**
Club MEDINA + Urban Mobilities
09.21.2009

**Tournament // 2009 Ping
Pong**
Asia GSD
Inflatables
10.16–11.06.2009

**Symposium //
Materiality + Construction:
5 Positions in Contemporary
Swiss Architecture**
Harvard European Design Circle
+ Harvard GSD + GSD Culture
Club
11.17.2009

**Seminar // Design Initiative
for Youth (DiY)**
Project Link
fall 2009

**Seminar // PROJECT LINK:
Summer High School Career
Discovery Program**
Project Link
07.06–07.31.2009

Seminar // LINK LiTE
Project Link
spring 2010

Winter Term // J-Term
Student Form + Student
Services   winter 2010

Mentorship // Peer Advisors
Student Form
school year 2009 - 2010

Inflatables // Korea GSD // LandGSD // Landscape Provocations & Practices // Latin GSD // MDesS Club // New Geographies // Out Design // Project Link/Design Initiative Youth // GSD Real Estate Development Club // SoCA (Social Change and Activism) // Student Experience Lecture Series // Student Exhibition Wall // Trays // Tourism Club // Urban Mobilities // Women in Design // Yoga GSD

Drew Gilpin Faust, President of Harvard University
Mohsen Mostafavi Dean of the Graduate School of Design

Martin Bechthold Co-Director of the Master in Design Studies Program
Eve Blau Director of the Master in Architecture Programs
Preston Scott Cohen Chair of the Department of Architecture
K. Michael Hays Associate Dean for Academic Affairs, Co-Director of Doctoral Programs
Alex Krieger Interim Chair of the Department of Urban Planning and Design
Sanford Kwinter Co-Director of the Master in Design Studies Program
Andrea Leers Director of the Master in Urban Design Degree Programs
Judith Grant Long Director of the Master in Urban Planning Degree Program
Antoine Picon Co-Director of Doctoral Programs
Charles Waldheim Chair of the Department of Landscape Architecture
Christian Werthmann Director of the Master in Landscape Architecture Degree Programs

Alan Altshuler Ruth and Frank Stanton Professor of Urban Policy and Planning and Harvard University Distinguished Service Professor
John Beardsley Adjunct Professor of Landscape Architecture
Martin Bechthold Professor of Architectural Technology and Co-Director of the Master in Design Studies Program
 and Technology Platform Coordinator
Pierre Bélanger Associate Professor of Landscape Architecture
Anita Berrizbeitia Professor of Landscape Architecture
Eve Blau Adjunct Professor of Architectural History and Director of the Master in Architecture Programs
Joan Busquets Martin Bucksbaum Professor in Practice of Urban Planning and Design
Holly Clarke Associate Professor of Landscape Architecture
Preston Scott Cohen Gerald M. McCue Professor in Architecture and Chair of the Department of Architecture
Felipe Correa Assistant Professor of Urban Design
Leland Cott Adjunct Professor of Urban Design
Danielle Etzler Assistant Professor of Architecture
Susan Fainstein Professor of Urban Planning
Richard T.T. Forman Professor of Advanced Environmental Studies in the Field of Landscape Ecology
Jose Gomez-Ibanez Derek Bok Professor of Urban Planning and Public Policy
Toni Griffin Adjunct Associate Professor of Urban Planning
K. Michael Hays Eliot Noyes Professor in Architectural Theory and Associate Dean for Academic Affairs and Co-Director of Doctoral Programs
Gary Hilderbrand Adjunct Professor of Landscape Architecture
John Hong Adjunct Associate Professor of Architecture
Timothy Hyde Assistant Professor of Architecture
Mariana Ibanez Assistant Professor of Architecture
Dorothée Imbert Associate Professor of Landscape Architecture
Jerold S. Kayden Frank Backus Williams Professor of Urban Planning and Design
Niall Kirkwood Professor of Landscape Architecture
Remment Koolhaas Professor in Practice of Architecture and Urban Design
Alex Krieger Professor in Practice of Urban Design and Interim Chair of the Department of Urban Planning and Design
Sanford Kwinter Professor of Architectural Theory and Criticism and Co-Director of the Master in Design Studies Program
Mark Laird Senior Lecturer in the History of Landscape Architecture
Andrea Leers Adjunct Professor of Architecture and Urban Design and Director of the Master in Urban Design Degree Programs
Jonathan Levi Adjunct Professor of Architecture
Judith Grant Long Assistant Professor of Urban Planning and Director of the Master in Urban Planning Degree Program
Joseph MacDonald Associate Professor of Architecture
Rodolfo Machado Professor in Practice of Architecture and Urban Design
Paula Meijerink Assistant Professor of Landscape Architecture
Michael Meredith Associate Professor of Architecture
Rafael Moneo Josep Lluis Sert Professor in Architecture
Toshiko Mori Robert P. Hubbard Professor in the Practice of Architecture
Mohsen Mostafavi Dean of the Graduate School of Design and Alexander and Victoria Wiley Professor of Design
Farshid Moussavi Professor in Practice of Architecture
Mark Mulligan Adjunct Associate Professor of Architecture
Erika Naginski Associate Professor of Architectural History
Richard Peiser Michael D. Spear Professor of Real Estate Development
Antoine Picon G. Ware Travelstead Professor of the History of Architecture and Technology and Co-Director of Doctoral Programs
Spiro Pollalis Professor of Design Technology and Management
Chris Reed Adjunct Associate Professor of Landscape Architecture
Christoph Reinhart Associate Professor of Architectural Technology

Ingeborg Rocker Assistant Professor of Architecture

Peter Rose Adjunct Professor of Architecture

Peter G. Rowe Raymond Garbe Professor of Architecture and Urban Design

A. Hashim Sarkis Aga Khan Professor of Landscape Architecture and Urbanism in Muslim Societies

Daniel L. Schodek Kumagai Research Professor of Architectural Technology

Thomas Schroepfer Associate Professor of Architecture

Matthias Schuler Adjunct Professor of Environmental Technology

Martha Schwartz Professor in Practice of Landscape Architecture

Mack Scogin Kajima Professor in Practice of Architecture

Jorge Silvetti Nelson Robinson Jr. Professor in Architecture

Christine Smith Robert C. and Marian K. Weinberg Professor of Architectural History

Carl Steinitz Alexander and Victoria Wiley Research Professor of Landscape Architecture and Planning

John R. Stilgoe Robert and Lois Orchard Professor in the History of Landscape Development

Kostas Terzidis Associate Professor of Architecture

Maryann Thompson Adjunct Professor of Architecture

Michael Van Valkenburgh Charles Eliot Professor in Practice of Landscape Architecture

Charles Waldheim John E. Irving Professor of Landscape Architecture and Chair of the Department of Landscape Architecture

Christian Werthmann Associate Professor of Landscape Architecture and Director of the Master in Landscape Architecture Degree Programs

T. Kelly Wilson Adjunct Associate Professor of Architecture

VISITING FACULTY

Iñaki Abalos Design Critic in Architecture and Design Critic in Urban Planning and Design

Frank Apesech Lecturer in Urban Planning and Design

Bridget Baines Design Critic in Landscape Architecture

George Baird Visiting Professor in Architecture

Shigeru Ban Visiting Professor in Architecture

Henri Bava Design Critic in Landscape Architecture

Nathaniel Belcher Visiting Associate Professor in Architecture

Eric Belsky Lecturer in Urban Planning and Design

Brian Blaesser Lecturer in Urban Planning and Design

Michael Blier Design Critic in Landscape Architecture

Sibel Bozdogan Lecturer in Architecture

Armando Carbonell Lecturer in Urban Planning and Design

Steven Cecil Design Critic in Urban Planning and Design

Edwin Chan Design Critic in Architecture

Suzanne Charles Lecturer in Urban Planning and Design

Betsy Colburn Lecturer in Landscape Architecture

Nazneen Cooper Lecturer in Landscape Architecture

Paul Cote Lecturer in Landscape Architecture and Urban Planning and Design

Pierre de Meuron Arthur Rotch Design Critic in Architecture

Peter Del Tredici Lecturer in Landscape Architecture

Jill Desimini Design Critic in Landscape Architecture

Richard Dimino Lecturer in Urban Planning and Design

William Doebele Frank Backus Williams Professor of Urban Planning and Design, Emeritus

Gareth Doherty Instructor in Landscape Architecture

Susannah Drake Design Critic in Landscape Architecture

Bill Dunster Lecturer in Architecture

Yael Erel Design Critic in Architecture

Stephen Ervin Lecturer in Landscape Architecture

Yvonne Farrell Kenzo Tange Visiting Design Critic in Architecture

Marc Fornes Lecturer in Architecture

Scheri Fultineer Design Critic in Landscape Architecture

David Gamble Design Critic in Urban Planning and Design

Andreas Georgoulias Lecturer in Architecture

Shauna Gillies-Smith Design Critic in Landscape Architecture

Geoffrey Goldberg Design Critic in Urban Planning and Design

Charles Harris Professor of Landscape Architecture, Emeritus

Jacques Herzog Arthur Rotch Design Critic in Architecture

Eelco Hooftman Design Critic in Landscape Architecture

Eric Howeler Design Critic in Architecture

Chris Hoxie Lecturer in Architecture

Jane Hutton Lecturer in Landscape Architecture

Louisa Hutton Design Critic in Architecture

Florian Idenburg Design Critic in Architecture

Richard Jennings Lecturer in Architecture

Gerhard Kallmann Professor Emeritus in Architecture
Ken Kao Lecturer in Architecture
Hanif Kara Lecturer in Architecture
Brian Kenet Lecturer in Landscape Architecture
Matt Kiefer Lecturer in Urban Planning and Design
Wooyoung Kimm Lecturer in Architecture
Gordon Kipping Design Critic in Architecture
David Leatherbarrow Lecturer in Landscape Architecture
Jennifer Lee Design Critic in Urban Planning and Design
George L. Legendre Design Critic in Architecture
Nina-Marie Lister Visiting Professor in Urban Planning and Design
John Macomber Lecturer in Architecture
Kathryn Madden Design Critic in Urban Planning and Design
David Mah Lecturer in Landscape Architecture
Edward Marchant Lecturer in Urban Planning and Design
Patrick McCafferty Lecturer in Architecture
Gerald McCue Professor in Urban Planning and Design, Emeritus
Anne McGhee Lecturer in Landscape Architecture
Shelley McNamara Kenzo Tange Visiting Design Critic in Architecture
Achim Menges Visiting Professor in Architecture
Emily Mueller De Celis Lecturer in Landscape Architecture
Glenn Mueller Lecturer in Urban Planning and Design
Ciro Najle Design Critic in Landscape Architecture and Urban Planning and Design
Paul Nakazawa Lecturer in Architecture
John Nastasi Lecturer in Architecture
Peter North Lecturer in Landscape Architecture
Valerio Olgiati Kenzo Tange Visiting Professor in Architecture
Cynthia Ottchen Design Critic in Architecture
Iinhee Park Lecturer in Architecture
Katherine Parsons Lecturer in Landscape Architecture
Cecilia Puga Design Critic in Architecture
Matthias Sauerbruch Design Critic in Architecture
Allen Sayegh Lecturer in Architecture
Veronika Schmid Lecturer in Architecture
Jeffrey Schnapp Visiting Professor in Architecture
Daniel L. Schodek Research Professor
Michael Schroeder Lecturer in Architecture
Rafael Segal Design Critic in Urban Planning and Design
Eduard Sekler Professor in Architecture, Emeritus
Frederick Smith Professor in Landscape Architecture, Emeritus
Ken Smith Design Critic in Landscape Architecture
Laura Solano Lecturer in Landscape Architecture
Kathy Spiegelman Design Critic in Urban Planning and Design
Jelena Srebric Lecturer in Architecture
James Stockard Lecturer in Urban Planning and Design
Hailim Suh Lecturer in Architecture
Nanako Umemoto Design Critic in Architecture
Matthew Urbanski Lecturer in Landscape Architecture
Francois Vigier Charles Dyer Norton Professor of Regional Planning, Emeritus
Emily Waugh Lecturer in Landscape Architecture
Elizabeth Whittaker Design Critic in Architecture
James Wickersham Lecturer in Architecture
Cameron Wu Design Critic in Architecture
Kongjian Yu Visiting Professor in Urban Planning and Design

LOEB FELLOWS

Ulrich H. Beck
Robert Bleiberg
Patricia L. Brown
Julie Campoli
Michael Creasey
Jose De Filippi
Donna Graves
Weiwen Huang
Gil Kelley
Neal Morris
Peter Steinbrueck

Jane Acheson Dean's Office
Patricia Alves Executive Education
Robert Angilly Public Services
Alla Armstrong Academic Finance
Lauren Baccus Human Resources
Kermit F. Baker Joint Center for Housing Studies
Pamela H. Baldwin Joint Center for Housing Studies
Lauren L. Beath Finance Office
Eric Belsky Joint Center for Housing Studies
P. Todd Belton Computer Resources
Susan Boland-Kourdov Computer Resources
Dan Borelli Exhibitions
Stacy Buckley Academic Services
Leslie Burke Dean's Office
Kevin Cahill Building Services
Bonnie Campbell Development
Susie Chung Joint Center for Housing Studies
Anna Cimini Computer Resources
Douglas Cogger Computer Resources
Ellen Colleran Landscape Architecture
Sean Conlon Registrar
Paul B. Cote Computer Resources
Anne Creamer Career Services
Andrea Croteau Architecture
Maria Da Rosa Technical Services
Mary Daniels Special Collections
Zhu X. Di Joint Center for Housing Studies
Sarah Dickinson Collections
Kathryn Eaton Human Resources
Barbara Elfman Advanced Studies Programs
Stephen M. Ervin Computer Resources
Angela Flynn Joint Center for Housing Studies
Heather A. Gallagher Executive Education
Keith Gnoza Financial Assistance
Meryl Golden Academic and Student Services
Desiree A. Goodwin Public Services
Irina Gorstein Library
Hal Gould Computer Resources
Laurel Gourd Joint Center for Housing Studies
Norton Greenfeld Development
Arin Gregorian Academic Finance
Deborah Grohe Building Services
Gail Gustafson Admissions
Mark Hagen Computer Resources
Barry J. Harper Building Services
Jill Harrington Admissions
Amanda Heighes Publications
Jackie Hernandez Joint Center for Housing Studies
Stephen Hickey Building Services
Megan A. Homan Development
Maggie Janik User Services
Anne Jeffko Human Resources
Nancy Jennings Executive Education
Johanna Kasubowski Visual Resources
Adam Kellie Library
Brooke Lynn King Events
Linda Kitch Library
Karen Kittredge Finance Office
Jeffrey Klug Career Discovery
Mary C. Lancaster Joint Center for Housing Studies
B. Kevin Lau Library
Sharon M. Lembo Real Estate Academic Initiative
Mary MacLean Finance Office
Daniel T. McCue Joint Center for Housing Studies

Michael McGrath Faculty Planning
Margaret Moore De Chicojay Executive Education
Corlette Moore McCoy Executive Education
Maria Moran Advanced Studies Programs
Maria A. Murphy Student Services
Gerilyn Nederhoff Admissions
Howard Nelson Technical Services
Natalie Newcom Development
Margaret Nipson Joint Center for Housing Studies
Bradley D. Niskanen User Services
Trevor O'Brien Building Services
Hannah T. Peters External Relations
Jacqueline Piracini Academic Services
Pilar Raynor Jordan Academic Finance
Julia Reiskind Visual Resources
Ann Renauer Finance Office
Carlos Reyes Student Services
Patricia Roberts Academic and Student Services
Kathleen Ryan External Relations
Meghan Ryan Harvard Design Magazine
William S. Saunders Harvard Design Magazine
Paul M. Scannell Building Services
Emily Scudder Technical Services
Laura Snowdon Student Services
Shannon Stecher Exhibitions
James Stockard Loeb Fellowship
Jennifer Swartout Architecture
Aimee Taberner Academic Administration
Kelly Teixeira Student Services
Julia Topalian Development
Ashley Torr Architecture
Jennifer Vallone Finance Office
Edna Van Saun Landscape Architecture
Melissa Vaughn Publications
Jessica Walton Real Estate Academic Initiative
Hugh Wilburn Library
Sara Wilkinson Human Resources
Abbe Will Joint Center for Housing Studies
Cameron Willard Building Services
Janet Wysocki Executive Education
Sarah Young Loeb Fellowship
Ines Zalduendo Library

Mohsen Mostafavi Dean of the Faculty of Design
Charles Waldheim Chair, Department of Landscape Architecture
Preston Scott Cohen Chair, Department of Architecture
Alex Krieger Interim Chair, Department of Urban Planning and Design
K. Michael Hays Co-Director of Doctoral Programs
Antoine Picon Co-Director of Doctoral Programs
Martin Bechtold Co-Director of the Master in Design Studies Program
Sanford Kwinter Co-Director of the Master in Design Studies Program

Emily Waugh Faculty Editor
Jennifer French (MArch I 2011) Editor
Bailey Kinkel (MLA I 2011) Editor
Diane M. Lipovsky (MLA I 2010) Editor
Amanda Heighes Copy Editor
Anita Kan Model Photography (unless otherwise noted)
Shannon Stecher Art Collector

IMAGE CREDITS

M. Iman Ansari
Jacob Belcher
Joseph Bergen
Cathy De Almeida
Anita Kan
Mary Kocol
Justin Knight
Evangelos Kotsioris
Kyun-Sun Lee
Dave Neault
Aaron Orenstein
Jon Sargent
Kris Snibbe
Ion Sokhos
Laura Viklund
James Willeford
Julia Xiao

ACKNOWLEDGMENTS

The Publication would not be possible
without the efforts of the following people:
Jane Acheson, Todd Belton, Dan Borelli,
Stacy Buckley, Doug Cogger, Ellen Colleran,
Sean Conlon, Felipe Correa, Andrea Croteau,
Barbara Elfman, Stephen Ervin, Hal Gould,
Mark Hagen, Jane Hutton, Maggie Janik,
Brooke Lynn King, Jared May, Mike McGrath,
Brad Niskanen, Trevor O'Brien, Pat Roberts,
Meghan Ryan, Paul Scannell, Dave Stuart,
Ashley Torr, Edna Van Saun, Melissa Vaughn,
Christian Werthmann, and all of the faculty,
staff, and students who have generously
shared their time and their work with us.

IMPRINT

Published by
Harvard University Graduate School
of Design, Actar

Graphic design and production
ActarBirkhäuserPro

GSD Platform 3 represents selected studios,
seminars, research, events, and exhibitions
from the 2009-2010 academic year.

For additional information and a more comprehensive selection of student work see
www.gsd.harvard.edu/studioworks

The Harvard Graduate School of Design is
a leading center for the education, information, and technical expertise on the built
environment. Its Departments of Architecture,
Landscape Architecture, and Urban Planning
and Design offer masters and doctoral degree programs, and provide the foundation for
the school's Advanced Studies and Executive
Education programs.

© of this edition, Harvard University Graduate
School of Design and Actar
© of the works, 2010 President
and Fellows of Harvard College
All rights reserved.

ISBN 978-84-92861-50-7
DL B-34.364-2010

DISTRIBUTION

ActarBirkhäuserD
Barcelona–Basel–New York
www.actarbirkhauser-d.com

Roca i Batlle 2
E-08023 Barcelona
T +34 93 417 49 93
F +34 93 418 67 07
salesbarcelona@actarbirkhauser.com

Viaduktstrasse 42
CH-4051 Basel
T +41 61 5689 800
F +41 61 5689 899
salesbasel@actarbirkhauser.com

151 Grand Street, 5th floor
New York, NY 10013
T +1 212 966 2207
F +1 212 966 2214
salesnewyork@actarbirkhauser.com